# Your Body: Gateway to the Divine

First published by O Books, 2009
O Books is an imprint of John Hunt Publishing Ltd., The Bothy, Deershot Lodge, Park Lane, Ropley,
Hants, SO24 0BE, UK
office1@o-books.net
www.o-books.net

Distribution in:

UK and Europe
Orca Book Services
orders@orcabookservices.co.uk
Tel: 01202 665432 Fax: 01202 666219
Int. code (44)

USA and Canada
NBN
custserv@nbnbooks.com
Tel: 1 800 462 6420 Fax: 1 800 338 4550

Australia and New Zealand
Brumby Books
sales@brumbybooks.com.au
Tel: 61 3 9761 5535 Fax: 61 3 9761 7095

Far East (offices in Singapore, Thailand,
Hong Kong, Taiwan)
Pansing Distribution Pte Ltd
kemal@pansing.com
Tel: 65 6319 9939 Fax: 65 6462 5761

South Africa
Alternative Books
altbook@peterhyde.co.za
Tel: 021 555 4027 Fax: 021 447 1430

Text copyright Josephine Chia 2008

Design: Stuart Davies

ISBN: 978 1 84694 177 1

A CIP catalogue record for this book is available
from the British Library.

Printed by Digital Book Print

O Books operates a distinctive and ethical publishing philosophy in
all areas of its business, from its global network of authors to
production and worldwide distribution.
This book is produced on FSC certified stock, within ISO14001
standards. The printer plants sufficient trees each year through
the Woodland Trust to absorb the level of emitted carbon in
its production.

# Your Body: Gateway to the Divine

Josephine Chia

BOOKS

Winchester, UK
Washington, USA

# CONTENTS

If you want to know what you were doing in your Past Life,
look at what your present body is like now
If you want to know what will happen to you in your
Future Life,
look at what your present mind is doing now

Tibetan saying

# Welcome and Introduction

If you are reading this, you are already awakened.

You could well be on the road to discovering the True Purpose in your Life. When you picked up this book, you may be simply looking for fellow travellers or you may still be seeking confirmation that you are on the right path. Then again, you might be a complete novice, newly receiving glimmers of insight to a purpose and way of life that is different from the one that you are living now. Whatever. Whichever. Welcome!

There is nothing new in this book.

Don't be put off by the above statement. It simply means that what *IS* already *IS*. What is new is the way you are choosing to see things, the way you are now open and ready to absorb what is being presented to you. Your inner eye has widened. Whether it stays open permanently is up to you, depending on whether you see with it enough. (Chapter 11 on the 6<sup>th</sup> Chakra will help you to maintain it at your optimum level.) Everything old, everything that had been viewed as staid or ordinary is now seen with a new perception. So the whole of your life is given new sparkle and becomes an adventure of discovery. The 15<sup>th</sup> Century Indian poet and mystic, Kabir said, "When the eyes and ears are open, even the leaves on the trees teach like pages from the scriptures"

## Be Your Own Authority

You and you alone are the only one to experience the Truth.

You are the Traveller, the Explorer. Others, like myself, can only tell you what we have seen, what we have experienced or what we are interpreting. But only you can test if what we say is accurate or the Truth. Be your own authority. Don't take on board anything that does not sit well in your heart. You can only believe it when you yourself know it to be true. Spiritual truth is not based on faith, it is a fact, a fact which you personally verify for yourself and can comprehend when the right ingredients are present. What stops us from perceiving the Truth is a kind of blindness. This blindness is a result of our over-focus on what we perceive as Reality. Remember the horses who had blinkers strapped to their bridle to prevent sideways vision? Well, our limited focus is like that. We prevent ourselves from having a vision of something greater, our limited focus prevents us from having a vision of The Divine in us and all about us. So it is time to remove your own blinkers.

Different teachers have different approaches and sometimes one approach suits you better than another. So although many different teachers have been saying the same thing, it is possible that you may find that you suddenly *get it* when a particular teacher explains a concept in a way that you can relate to. Cobwebs that have shielded you from *The Light* are suddenly swept away by that particular teacher due to his/her ability to explain. Or you have swept away your own cobwebs to see beyond words. Kahlil Gibran, the Lebanese poet and writer said in *The Prophet, Wisdom is not in words but in the meaning within words*. So maybe some words have more meaning to you now than previously. Or perhaps your circumstances have changed making you more receptive. Quite often, a repeated sorrow or crisis could act as a trigger. Paulo Coelho, in his book, *Like The Flowing River*, told the story of a pencil. He said that the pencil has to endure some pain, (ie when we sharpen a pencil), in order for it to become sharper. (ie becoming useful or with better vision) Remember the story in the bible about the Sower sowing seeds? Not all the seeds fell in the right place so those could not be germinated. The moment you choose to question the depth and meaning of your life, it means some seeds have fallen in the right part of the ground. The moment you start questioning the authenticity of your life, you have begun your spiritual journey. Now all you need to do is to water and feed the seeds for them to grow into

2

healthy, living plants.

What any teacher says must not be taken as facts. *For them to become facts, you, yourself, must know them to be true.* And the only way for you to transform what other people say into facts is by your own experience. This means that what you learn is *not* book knowledge. It is *not* intellectual knowledge. It is knowledge gained from a deeply Intuitive Personal Experience. It is a First-Hand Experience from which you will emerge with no doubt of your Divinity, no doubt of the presence of The Divine Consciousness. A teacher's role is to provide the framework and the foothold for you to cross the bridge into the spiritual realm. The framework and foothold may vary from teacher to teacher. You have to decide which is the best method for you. Trust me – there is no One Method. Don't let anyone lay claim to their singular method at the expense of others. Ordained Vedic Priest and Mantra Teacher, Thomas Ashley-Farrand (aka Namadeva) said in reference to spiritual paths "There are words that make me crazy: *The Only, Highest, Best, Fastest.* Humanity is very diverse, like an orchestra. We need only to find the appropriate instrument for our development." You may have observed that usually those who become too evangelical and feel they have to defend their own method and belittle all others are insecure. They are also the same people who kill others to defend their own beliefs. No real spiritual learning can be based on insecurity, fear or violence. The latter three emotions can be a springboard but not a path. Remember that you and only you can put the foot forward over that chasm.

## Shift your View-Point and Make the Connection to the Divine

However, don't be stagnated by old-outdated viewpoints. Be prepared to step out of your comfort zone. Metaphorically, climb new mountains to change your view. The *Truth Out There* or *The Truth of The Divine Consciousness* is a huge concept. It is not like a small single flower that we can hold in one hand or see with our physical eyes. Imagine trying to see the whole of Alaska or the Earth from one view-point like from one mountain in the *Alps, Rockies, Himalayas* or wherever you happened to be standing. You cannot grasp the hugeness of the place until you are overhead, way overhead, like in the sky or way out of the confines of Earth, from a point in space. In the same way, to understand the enormity of the Divine Consciousness, you need to shift your view-point, move away from the confines of your small mind, your restrictive intellect. You learn to use your Intuition which is not limited by the forms of your body and mind, to enable you to perceive the Divine Consciousness.

Only then, from this personal experiential understanding can you discover why you are here on this Earth and what you are meant to fulfil. You come laden with gifts and talents that are your very own. No other person has that same set of gifts. When you are expressing those gifts, you are not being selfish, you are expressing the Divine here on Earth and you are contributing to society in your own, unique way. (The section on *Transforming Yourself Is Your Service To The World* in the final chapter of this book talks further about this.) In actual fact, if you don't express those gifts, you are thwarting the Divine from working through you.

Once you have established a link to The Divine, you will no longer be the same, your perception of this world will not be the same. Everything that you see and experience can stir your heart and bring you great joy, something as simple as the sight of a flower or tree, the colour of the sky or moon, the giggle of a child. You become truly alive, and like Kabir say, everything teaches you something. Your life will be enhanced by this Aladdin's cave of spiritual knowledge that you are now privy to. The more you visit this site, as you do to a modern website on the computer, the more established you will become in making the link or connection. It's like book-marking your favourite site to return to. Eventually, with a lot of practice, it is this connection with The Divine that will bring you the peace and happiness you seek – everyone here on Earth seeks, whether they know it or not. This kind of happiness is not necessarily the *Hip! Hip Hurrah!* variety though it can be sometimes but it is a long-lasting sustaining type which fills you with such a deep joy that nothing external that is bad, disappointing or negative can eradicate. The Divine connection will inform your life so that whatever you do, your ego personality is relegated to the station it is meant to be, that of servant to the Spiritual You.

## Don't be a Spiritual Arm-Chair Traveller

Liken your spiritual journey to that of a journey on the physical plane.

There are travellers before you who have been to places you may not have been. People might write articles, travel brochures or books about the places they visited. They might describe the beauty, the landscape, the indigenous people, their customs and foods, the fauna and flora. The place could be the rugged wind-swept Cape Wrath in Western Scotland or the wilderness of Alaska, Yukon or Australia; the teeming humanity in India, Hong Kong or Singapore, the tropical jungles of Borneo or Papua New Guinea. You might have seen images or films of one of these places, you might even get a fairly good sense of what it might be like, its temperature, its geographical features, its places of interests. It is possible that with the advancement in technology, you could probably experience a virtual journey to that place. But until you yourself actually make a visit, you will never really know what it is like. Your idea of that place is still *second-hand* until you yourself make that visit. You can only truly experience by being there. It is exactly the same with a spiritual journey.

It is possible that you are not *really* that interested in going to other places. Or it is possible that you genuinely want to know things but do not wish to leave your comfort zone to put on hiking boots, live in a tent, climb over rugged mountains or canoe down a crocodile-populated river or trek through a mosquito-infested forest or swamp, or cope with below-zero temperatures to experience a place first-hand. So you experience them on the fringe, just dabbling, like going on holiday when someone else tells you where to go, what to see, what to eat. Or you remain an arm-chair traveller totally. You read the relevant books, watch programmes on the *Discovery Channel*, the *History Channel*, or maybe some so-called *Reality Programmes*. Whatever you choose to do is a choice

But this means that you can only *talk* about places with information and knowledge *others* gave you; with perceptions that others perceived, with opinions that others opined. Everything is gained second-hand. You might use the language of travel, talk with some authority, may even appear well-informed but you still haven't been there. These days with digital photography and computer trickery, you can even frame yourself against a backdrop of a place you have never been to: *Paris, Leaning Tower of Pisa, Great Wall of China*, etc. If you wanted to, you could even fool some people into thinking you had been there, send them a postcard from there. (Actually, there is a computer company offering this service. You send them your photo and they generate your image onto a picture of the place of your choice and they even stick a stamp of that country and then you can send it to your friends.) You could be photographed poised over a tiger you were supposed to have killed or could have been wrestling with a crocodile or on a bronco horse or kayaking through wild, white water rapids. Photographs can lie – and do lie these days. You don't have to be there at all. That is your choice of course. But then you cannot make genuine comments or pass any judgment of places you have not truly visited.

Therefore, the people who say, God (or The Divine Consciousness) does not exist may not have travelled to the right place to find out. Next time someone makes such a statement, ask him if he had actually made a spiritual journey to find out. Don't be deterred by negative soothsayers. These people are numerous. Because they can't be bothered with spiritual practices, which can be hard work sometimes (no one says it will be easy peasy), they try to disillusion others too. Take no notice. If you want to find out the truth, you will.

If I say to you that there is a sign that said *Population of Chicken, Alaska: 26 and one old grump,* you might say the sign does not exist. Even if I showed you the photograph of the sign I had taken whilst I was there, you could say that I faked it. So the only way to find out if I am really telling the truth is for you to go visit the place.

So it is the same with a spiritual journey.

How committed are you to finding True Peace and Happiness? How important is it to you to discover the True You or The Divine? How far are you prepared to leave your padded, luxurious sofa? An understanding of The Divine, of *The Truth Out There* will not drop into your lap like a parcel that has been Fedex, DHL, Parcel Post or whatever. It's a trip you have to make – if you want to be happy, if you want to be peaceful, if you want to see beyond the trappings of what we designate as *Life* so that you can discover the Real Truth.

## Past Spiritual Explorers

Though we have to experience the place ourselves, do the journey ourselves, we are very, very lucky because we no longer have to blaze trails. This is the beauty of it. Others who have gone before you had set dynamites to the obstructions before you, cleared the rocks, sweep-clean the tangled jungle. In spiritual travel, these paths were forged by the Past Spiritual Explorers, those whom we call Enlightened Beings – the Masters, Gurus, Sages, Prophets, Saints. I am sure you know some of the names: Jesus, Buddha, Mohammed, Khalil Gibran, Guru Nanak, Saint Teresa, Lao Tze and others, too numerous to mention. They were the Spiritual

7

Map Makers, the ones who set up directional boards, drew up warning signs of pitfalls, sheer cliffs, dangerous creatures. What they offer us is information, alternative routes, easier routes, (figuratively) what type of equipment we should take, what kind of supplies we need on our journey, what type of constitution we need to possess to enable us to complete our journey. Of course there are modern, living Teachers too, who continue to give us their wisdom so that we may find our way out of the maze of our problems: The Dalai Lama, Swami Satchidananda, Eckhart Tolle, Thich Nhat Hanh and so many others.

It is important to understand the fact that all these different Spiritual Explorers are birthed from different geographical premises and landscapes, different nationalities and cultures, different social and historical milieu. This will invariably mean that the paths they offer might vary. Each of their teachings will be based on words and customs of their relevant culture. This does not make any particular teaching less or more – just different. Sometimes the difference might appeal because of its exoticness and difference, other times not. The important thing is to be open and to choose a path that resonates with you at your particular stage of development. Of course, one has to be wary of the path we choose too, one has to choose it with our intuition, not our mind. Choosing the wrong path can have its consequences. When Scott and Edmudsen and their expedition teams were racing to the South Pole, both took different routes. But their destination was the same. Both teams made it to the Pole, one slower than the other. In the end, all Spiritual Quests result in the same. It is only the path which differs but choose it with care to ensure that you have sufficient energy and supplies for your journey. (The latter was Scott's miscalculation and cause of his team's demise.) What path you choose depends on your temperament and the equipment you possess. It is only the fearful and the fundamentalists that claim that theirs is the only True Path.

Reading all about these things, gathering all the useful information still doesn't make you a traveller.

Ultimately, you have to make the journey yourself.

## Who am I to Write This Book?

Don't make the mistake of thinking that just because I am writing a book, I know everything or am perfect. Far from it. It is my imperfection and my humanity that makes me want to share my journey with you because I know how far I have fallen. I have felt the jagged rocks, have experienced stones being thrown at me, have been choked by the foul fumes of negativity, been assailed by despair and sadness. But I know I am truly fortunate because in my darkest moments, there was always a beam of Light that shone on me to guide me through, Light in the form of caring people, helpful friends and Spiritual Teachers, both Earthly and Astrally, even good, relevant books. I know it is possible to recapture the True Meaning of life because some others have held out a helping hand to me. And I hope that by writing this, I too can proffer a helping hand for those who might need one. I have moved from extreme poverty to extreme wealth and then back to moderate poverty. I have been separated from my children and my family, limped through two marriages, suffered a cancer scare, moved to a different country and different culture, have understood what it meant to be truly alone, to be an alien and foreigner to someone else's culture and social mores. I have recently discovered that I cannot return to my native country to live because I had given up its citizenship for the man I love who in the end betrayed me.

Boy, have I made mistakes in this life-time! In Paulo Coelho's story of the pencil, he said that the pencil has five qualities. One of its qualities is "the pencil allows us to use an eraser to rub out any mistakes." His words made me feel less bad about my mistakes and my human frailty. Would I have been complacent if I did not make those mistakes? I have learnt that mistakes themselves can be our study points from which we can learn and improve. In my darkest moments – and there were plenty, I always trusted and believe in a Higher Purpose, a Higher Source and remain connected. This is not blind faith, it is holding the telephone line between The Divine and myself open so that The Divine can speak to me and pull me through the adversities that my karma necessitated that I had to experience. To reach this understanding that it is my own karma, that I myself had created, for all these things to happen to me was in itself a learning experience. A tough one to accept but nonetheless true. Once I had accepted it, I accepted my own part in it. I am responsible. And once I accepted responsibility, I started to feel less like a victim.

But why should you want to know this?

Because, you, like all other beings on this earth are looking for ways to make your life better. You want to be happy. Perhaps you feel that life is empty, has no meaning. You want to feel fulfilled. If you can see that it is possible for someone who went through the mills (and possibly, is still going through them) can cope because of my belief in a Higher Connection, then you too can cope and enhance your life by simply connecting. I am no great sage who has gone beyond the daily intrusions of life, I am still very much of the Earthly realm, an average person struggling in ordinary life to know and understand The Divine. That is why this book shows how spirituality at this level is pragmatic, how we can start with what we are and what we know to move towards making that connection to The Divine which will infuse our lives with Divine Light. We don't have to run away to any mountain cave, ashram or monastery to discover The Divine. We may need the occasional solitude to help us to re-tune and re-focus but essentially this book is about finding The Divine in our daily lives, in our Body, in our relationships and in nature.

I did not *just* survive my karma. To simply survive is to merely exist. I have discovered that it is possible to live life in a more conscious way, to live every moment in utter joy. I am not claiming that I am no longer beset by the demons of my human frailties but that on those occasions when the thunder clouds gather, I have learnt to seek shelter until the sun shines again. This is all I can offer you. I cannot even claim to be *Enlightened*. I am a Seeker of The Truth just the same as you are. I don't know all the answers and I won't be supplying you answers. These you will find for yourself when your connection to The Divine is forged strongly. All I can say is that I am only passing on what I am still learning, put in a form of my own to help make spiritual concepts clearer, help you see how spirituality is pragmatic, how it is an **essential** part of our daily life. In my work as a yoga therapist, doing mostly one-to-one work, I have learnt so much from my students, learnt so much about how the body expresses joy and pain and, more importantly, hidden sorrows. Learning to connect with The Divine will help you release those hidden sorrows and free you from any emotional issues that are clutching your body and mind in pain. This is because the process of connecting with your True Self and The Divine Consciousness is also a process of healing.

The latter was one of the things I learnt about myself on my own journey. There were huge stores of pain within myself that affected the way I saw myself and other people, thereby influencing my relationships. The first escape from the shards of pain was to become aware of them; and the second, was to let them go, the third is to heal by letting the Divine Light in. If you have to do this all by yourself, it is hard. I have learnt that you can call on The Divine to lighten the load. (Or fellow travellers like healers and therapists) The connection to The Divine is not a metaphysical process that requires faith but is a physical process that starts with becoming aware of your body, your mind. This is my experience. Perhaps writing about it will show you how important the body is towards understanding The Divine. I seem to be more aware than I was before, more clear than I had been before – and that makes me live my life in a positive way and with joy. If you need the authority of a sage or an Enlightened One, then it may not suit you to travel along the path I am taking. But that is okay too, I can understand. Every good fortune be with you on the path you are taking. But if you decide to walk along with me, I say *Welcome* and *Thank You* for letting me share with you!

## Postscript

I use The Body to indicate both body and mind so as not to have to repeat the words, the body and the mind. (In Sanskrit, this conglomerate of body+mind+psychological make-up is called *sharira*.) But to indicate the physical body itself, I will use the words in small case – the body.

The word *God* has so many different connotations for different people. In order not to get caught in semantics, I shall use the word *The Divine* or *Divine Consciousness* interchangeably to suggest this Higher Spiritual Aspect. This is not a prescriptive term but is a descriptive one. It need not be a being. It could just be a principle or worldview. Please view the term in the manner in which you are familiar and comfortable. This book does not purport to steer you towards any particular religion but to encourage you to recognise that The Divine is present whichever form you feel The Divine is expressed in. The Divine is present whether you link up with it or not. However this book, based on Eastern teachings, particularly, the different forms of yoga, will illustrate how The Divine is manifested in you. This philosophy operates on the belief that The Spiritual part of ourselves is our primary make-up and our physical body is our secondary make-up. Even if you don't subscribe to this, don't worry because the methods mentioned in this book will still help you to cope with life's adversities whether you believe or not believe in a Higher Source. But it is hoped that you can use what you have, The Body – which is you – as a gateway to towards understanding The Divine. You will learn techniques of making that connection as and when you need it so that you can receive the largest you are entitled to and be truly happy and peaceful.

Wishing you peace, happiness and a fulfilled life!

*Phine*

Josephine Chia

---

**Please Note:**

All exercises, physical, emotional and mental, in this book have to be practised safely and with full responsibility of your own body and your mind. Any suggested practices for particular conditions have to be used wisely and in conjunction with proper medical advice. If you should use any information in this book, which is your constitutional right, the author and publisher accept no responsibility for your actions.

# CHAPTER 1

# Living In Shadow

*"Without good health, you cannot achieve anything in the material world or the spiritual line. Good health is the most coveted possession of all."*
Swami Sivananda,
*Health and Hatha Yoga*

Our journey towards the Divine Consciousness is along the same road as that of our healing and our connection to others. When we are diseased, we are not whole. When we are not whole, it means parts of ourselves are in shadow, deprived of Spiritual Light, divorced from The Divine. Just like plants which cannot thrive without the physical sun, aspects of ourselves which are deprived of the Spiritual Sun shrivel, become diseased, then die. (We are not talking about physical diseases only but also emotional and mental diseases that can express themselves as physical diseases. However healing is more than a cure. Sometimes healing can take place without resulting in a cure. Sometimes a cure can occur without true healing.) When we move towards Spiritual Light, (some may call this *The Process of Enlightenment*) we are feeding on the nourishment that the Divine provides. As we bask in the qualities of the Divine, we become balanced, stronger, healthier and fitter. We become happy and fulfilled. We understand our own Divinity and we merge with the Universal Divinity. When we do so, our relationships with others on this planet are also better and healthier. That is why it is necessary for every single person to work on their spiritual growth.

There is no need to rely on faith or to take leaps of belief to understand The Divine. All you need is some time and effort to spend to return home to your Real Self. There is also no need to believe in me. I am not here to teach you anything, merely to share some understanding that will provide you with methods to discover your Real Self. The purpose of this book is to show you a practical way of getting to know yourself better and to be in touch with the Divine Consciousness.

## You are not alone.

Forgetting the existence of somebody does not mean the person is not there. If you had not contacted your parent, sibling or friend for a long while, it does not mean the person is gone – merely that your communication methods are not good. Perhaps you hadn't telephoned each other, wrote letters and emails or visited. So this book is about helping you to connect to an old friend – The Divine Consciousness. You are not alone. Regular practice will help you to sense this Greater Presence and further practice will help you to be in touch. This book will attempt to help you to make that connection and show how you can bring in the Light that will shine upon any shadow you may hold within you. It is a gradual process of unfoldment – the pace is yours to set. There is no competition.

## Your Body Is A Message Board

It is amazing how much your body is a sign board for what is going on inside you, emotionally, physically and mentally. A good therapist, including a yoga therapist, can read the messages your body is sending out. These messages are kind of your SOS signals. The Inner You is trying to catch your attention to what is going on at a deeper level which your Conscious Mind is either not picking up to or is unable to do so. You might find yourself suffering from a tension headache, backache, fear or phobia. More than not, these are symptoms, not the cause. Your body is suggesting to you that you should tackle the source of these ailments. Obviously, a quick-fix medication for many of these conditions is available and in many cases is necessary. However, too much reliance on medications without looking into the real cause of the problems will mean that you won't get rid of the conditions permanently. Getting rid of the symptoms does not remove the cause.

## Being Alert To The Body

Being alert to what your body is trying to tell you is not the same as being a hypochondriac. Being a hypochondriac means being overtly focused on every ache and pain in the body and indulging in the feelings about them by magnifying their problems. It is obsessive behaviour. A hypochondriac is seeking attention from others through their real or imagined ailments. Awareness is different. Awareness means bringing your attention to what is happening to you at this very moment, exactly NOW, not yesterday, not tomorrow, not later but NOW. This necessitates your mind being present, being here – and not somewhere else. Being Present and In-The-Now is not just a state but is also a process. When the Mind engages with the Present, it is as if *maya* or the veil of illusion is being peeled back bringing you clarity and happiness. A journalist once asked the Dalai Lama when his happiest moment was. The Dalai Lama pondered, then with his usual delightful chuckle, said, " I think Now."

The phrase *the Power Of Now* and such-like might be over-used these days and may become hackneyed but the concept is worth understanding because when you can truly be in the moment, great things happen.

Awareness means not shutting yourself out from the messages your body or mind is sending out so that you can make the necessary adjustments to make yourself easeful. You can be aware without being reactive. By doing so, you develop the ability to *witness* yourself. This ability is of such paramount importance towards understanding yourself that we will cover the topic again later when we discuss the 3$^{rd}$ and 6$^{th}$ Chakras or Gateways.

Easefulness in the body is also easefulness in the mind and emotions. This is the beauty of *Be*-ing. You are learning the art of awareness to know yourself better. Your physical body is the tool you have to begin your Self-Exploration, it is the expression of all that you are; everything that has happened to you, everything you have eaten or not eaten, everything you have done or not done for the health of your body, every thought you had, everything you ever said has given rise to this body in this present condition. This is the meaning of the Tibetan saying at the front of this book.

The latter concept might not be so easily conceivable if you believe in only this life-time. But it will still work. What you did as a child, as a teenager to your body will manifest itself when you are an adult. On the physical level, for instance, if you are a young athlete, your body could still be strong when you enter middle-age; if you had indulged in the wrong foods and had been obese as a child, you might suffer from certain conditions like diabetes, high blood pressure in your latter years, etc. On an emotional level, what your parents, teachers and people said about you and to you will affect the way you function as an adult. The way you are acting now may not be the True You, just someone who has been forced to become what you are.

If you subscribe to the view of having lived many lives, then some of your present ailments or conditions could have been a result of what you did in one of those life-times. This is the law of karma, of cause-and-effect. Karma is not a law wielded by some Dark God or Universal Presence but is a natural law similar to the *As you sow, so shall you reap* law. It is inescapable. You can't eat all the rubbish you craved and then expect that the body should not suffer its consequences. No such luck I'm afraid. The same thing will occur if you pollute your mind with negative or evil thoughts, your emotional make-up will be tainted.

No man is an island. This means an individual on this planet does not exist in complete isolation from others. Therefore our relationship with others also affect the way we are. On a physiological level, we inherit genes from our parents and grandparents and their parents before them. On an emotional and mental level, we also inherit and adopt certain attitudes, behavioural and cultural patterns from our forebears. Sometimes a bad habit, like a way of sitting, can be passed from generation to generation and then we come to believe that it is an inherited trait! Or we could have inherited an attitude, for instance if we disliked a particular race or a particular food, it could be that it was our family who generated that feeling. It needs someone in the family to break the chain of bad habit. Outside of our familial sphere, we are all inter-related to other beings who exist on this planet. What we are and have become is the growth embodiment of our actions and decisions in relation to others. There would have been alternative other-selves of ourselves who would have become something different if we had taken other actions and other decisions in the same circumstances but those selves did not come into being. Sometimes in the process of healing, we may have to revisit our past in a metaphysical way so that we could take the decisions we should have taken in the first place.

## Not Just Skin And Bones

We are not just skin and bones. You don't need to be an Enlightened Being to make this discovery. All it needs is for you to become more sensitive to what is happening to your physical body.

Personally, I took to yoga because I suffered from splitting headaches and many other things, not from any idea of being enlightened. I was amazed at the instant recovery from headaches just through one yoga session because of its excellent breathing techniques! When I had suspected ovarian cancer, my life changed. When you are faced with the possibility of degeneration or death, your life opens up in front of you. It was a moment of epiphany for me. Yoga helped me through all the difficult times. Although my journey began with physical or Hatha Yoga, it soon encompassed Raja Yoga which dealt with the ravages of the Mind. My interest in yoga and all its various forms was ignited and it grew and grew and it slowly led to the path that I am now travelling. As a matter of interest, yoga existed in India long before either Hinduism and Buddhism came about. Both these religions have incorporated yogic teachings into the fabric of their tenets. Gautama Buddha, the historical Buddha was a yogi first before he became a Buddha. Therefore much of his teachings and certain forms of yoga share some similarities and it might appear that yoga using the names of Hindu deities is Hindu-based. Yoga is based on the Vedas, the oldest scriptures in India and so is Hinduism, hence the similarities. Just as the Greeks use the mythology of their gods to present concepts and principles, so too does yoga use gods and deities to tell the story of Creation, bravery, purity etc. So although yoga, in general,  is spiritual, it is not religious. (Having said this, *Bhakti Yoga* means Devotional Yoga. Thus in its devotion to deities and Hindu Gods, there is a strong sense of religiosity.)

The beauty of it is that yoga is quite a pragmatic science and I found I could test out some of the claims of the great gurus, more than I could in other disciplines I have tried. I found that I don't have to take things on board unless I could verify them to some extent or at least be given direction towards that discovery.

Let me give you an example.

Let us say that someone told me about *Perth* in the North of Scotland or *Chicken* in Alaska. Let us say that I am not entirely convinced that either of those places exists but I am really interested and am willing to spend time to find out. So the person gives me excellent directions on how to get there. Whilst I am travelling, I become aware that the person really knows what he was talking about because I see the roads he mentioned, the towns I am passing, the fascinating landmarks, etc. The longer I spend on the road towards the place and the more that I see which concur with his description, the more I become convinced that the place he said existed will exist.

This is the same as a spiritual discovery. I am in that stage. The longer I am on the spiritual path, the more convinced I am that what the Spiritual Masters were talking about is true. I have not reached my destination yet but I have seen and experienced many things that have concurred with what they have taught, compelling enough for me to want to continue with my journey. So what I am sharing with you in this book are the landmarks and milestones which you too can verify for yourself. (Remember that your path does not have to be through yoga alone, this is only one of the many paths that are available.)

## Yoga – The Ultimate Union

The Indian Yogis knew that a system of Mind Exploration and Overcoming The Mind still has to begin with what we own – with the body. Mainly in the West, Hatha Yoga has almost become a *Keep Fit, Body Beautiful* system, with a bit of Meditation and Relaxation thrown in for good measure. In some methods of teaching, Hatha Yoga has degenerated into what I call *Gym Yoga*, a muscle and bone body work-out system focussed on the external rather than the internal and very goal-oriented. There is nothing wasteful with this because even at this gross level, the system greatly benefits the body and also the mind. But to assume that this is what the whole system of Yoga is about is to diminish the whole purpose of the true Yoga.

In actuality, the only true goal of yoga is the union of the body and mind in such a way that we discover our True Selves. The discovery of our True Self is the same discovery of the Divine Consciousness for we are not separate from it. Hatha Yoga is only one of the eightfold paths towards YOGA – that ultimate Union. Much of the teachings of the Ancient Sages and Gurus were passed on through the oral tradition. Patanjali, scholar, Sanskrit grammarian and philosopher (2nd Century BC) was credited with setting the teachings into a systematic order. This system enables the Seeker of Truth to ascertain the landmarks and milestones on the journey towards YOGA, its Sanskrit equivalent is *Yuj* – to unite, yoke.

The Eight-Fold Path is a serious and prolonged study unto itself and has been detailed in many good books and is well worth an examination if the inclination takes you. These eightfold paths are often interpreted as rungs on a ladder and many interpret them as us having to climb one rung after the other until we reach the ultimate rung of *Samadhi* or Enlightenment. I personally do not see it like this but instead view the eightfold path as simulta-neous levels of consciousness that we have to be aware of and adopt. Think of a tree with a strong trunk. The eight branches or limbs create the symmetry of the tree. The first two branches have to do with your attitude towards others and towards yourself. The eighth branch is the state of Enlightenment. Therefore at any one stage in our spiritual journey, we are holding all of the levels in our mind in varying degrees of development and completion. I am of the view that we can experience small bursts of *enlight-enment* which will propel us to that Big One someday. (We will talk more about this when we discuss the 7$^{th}$ or Crown Chakra.)

## Hatha Yoga

Hatha Yoga is on the third limb of Pantajali's Eightfold path. It is a scientific discipline which is developed from thousands of years of study into the body to increase your vitality in the body through the flow of *prana*. This is an important aspect of spiritual practices because as Swami Sivananda said in the quote at the top of this chapter, you could not achieve anything without good health. Spiritual practices require the stamina of a long distance runner because they take time and effort, not just one hour in a class per week. You would not consider running the marathon if you did not get into shape first. In the same way, hatha yoga prepares the body and Raja Yoga prepares the mind for the spiritual marathon.

Hatha yoga does this through the dynamics of *asanas*, generally translated as postures, where the body is put into various positions, not just for theatrical effect or as a form of gymnastics, but to trigger the chakras or energy centres that are held within the body. (More of this later in the chapter on *gateways* into the Energy or Pranic Body). To direct the *Pranic* Energy, like the creation of dams to reap hydroelectric power, hatha yoga is also about the effective use of *bandas* (generally translated as seals) and *mudras* (hand gestures) to generate and enhance your body's own electrical power. To clear your body of the bad stuff that has accumulated through years of bad practice, poor diet, negative thinking, etc., hatha yoga uses *kriyas* as cleansing techniques. (Swami Sivanananda's excellent book and many other books have been written on these three aspects of hatha yoga so I won't be elaborating here. They are mentioned here to show you that hatha yoga is not a shallow *keep fit* fad.) That is why in the true discipline of any of the paths of yoga, the real work is taking place inside you; hence outward posturing is neither its true purpose nor goal.

## Eastern Healing Method

Things are changing but generally, Western medicine treats symptoms, so if you have a headache, a pill is given to cure that headache. There are many advantages of Western medicine so this section is not casting any opinion on which is the better method between Western and Eastern methods of healing but just to show how Eastern healing takes place. This book does not ask nor persuade you to abandon conventional healing methods but to give you more information on how knowledge of the yogic system will help you to identify problem areas in your life and how to deal with them. Adopting a more holistic method, combining Western and Eastern methods might help you to reduce your medication and help you to take control of your ill health or illness. Western science and medical science have given us practical insights into our body and mind and it will be silly to ignore these.

Whether it is Indian or Chinese, the basis of tackling ailments, illness and diseases is to check the balance of body fluids and body energy. The focus is beyond muscles and bones, rather it is on a medium we call *prana* in Indian, *chi* in Chinese, *ki* in Japanese, *lung* in Tibetan, *angin* in Malay, the American Indians call it *Orenda* and the Polynesians call it *Mana*.. This is your Inner Vital Energy. Its ebb and flow is the thing that determines your health. There are very good books on this so I won't be elaborating too much here either although a further chapter will show you how you can utilise this. Suffice to say that most Eastern systems of exercise, like Yoga and Tai Chi are designed to influence the ebb and flow of your inner energy so that you will be at optimum health. As the Chinese words suggest, you will be at your Highest Energy level (*Tai* is Highest; *Chi* is Inner Energy).

The by-products of regular practises of hatha yoga is that you breathe well, so you sleep well and are more relaxed; your muscles become toned, your organs stay alive and energised as the movements in the postures send oxygen and nourishing blood to them, especially the brain; your joints are properly lubricated, you build up bone, etc.

Each form of yoga practice has arisen from Patanjali's *Eight Limbs*. You could achieve your unity through Bhakti (Devotional Yoga), Kundalini (Energy/Prana) Yoga, Jnana (Knowledge) Yoga and many others. Gurus for each of the paths varies too and each offer their own style and method. So your choice is dependent on your inclination and your constitution. But the goal remains the same – to enable you to reach an understanding of yourself and helping you to unite with the Divine Consciousness.

On an emotional level, the process of yogic practices helps you to release blockages and set you free. That is why the process of a spiritual discipline like yoga is also a process of healing.

**Something To Do (1):**

Take your pulse. You can do this anywhere and any time. On the bus, watching TV, waiting for someone, on the loo. Don't turn it into a big or medical issue. You don't really have to know how many beats you should have. It helps but it is not essential. Place your thumb or four fingers on the pulse at your wrist. Close your eyes. Focus till you can feel your pulse. How does it feel? Is it steady, fast or slow? Regular or irregular? This is how the river of your life is flowing. Just be in tune with it.

## CHAPTER 2

# One Single Step At A Time

*"Prana is the best tonic. Simple breathing can heal. Just divert that energy to work at wherever you have a problem."*
Swami Satchidananda,
*To Know Your self*

The Chinese philosopher, Kung Fu Tze says, "A journey of a thousand Li begins with the First Step." (*Li* is a Chinese mile). You might say that this is only logical. Why should it take a philosopher to come up with something so simple? Confucius, (which is the Latinised name of Kung Fu Tze) realised that people sometimes focus on the big or entire journey. This tendency to envisage the entire journey or task caused people to be daunted by its prospect. For example if you were planning to write a book of one hundred pages and you are on page 1 which is blank, it can be pretty scary, especially if you don't have a great deal of faith in yourself or confidence. If you have to run or walk a marathon, if you only think of the many miles ahead, you might be filled with the notion that you are incapable of finishing the journey. By showing us that we should shift our view-point and focus on the first step, which is a more manageable concept, we don't fill our mind with fear about *not* tackling the huge journey. Instead of saying, "Oh, I cannot walk a thousand miles," we can happily say, "Of course I can manage one single step." As you know, each single step adds to the next single step and so on – and if you persevere, you will complete a thousand miles. You take the first step and the rest of the journey will happen. Trust in yourself. Don't let fear cloud your judgement.

A spiritual journey is the same. Take one single step at a time.

From whatever spot you are standing, from wherever you are, physically, emotionally, mentally. Don't beat yourself up about the past, what you have done or where you have come from. There are ways to rectify the repercussions of your past actions which we will discuss in due course. If you are continually caught up in the past, you are wasting precious Vital Energy by locking your Energy in that past. Change begins from where you are at, the past has already happened. (In one of the techniques of going into the Past, you can take a salve to the situation though the situation itself cannot be undone. See the chapter on the 7$^{th}$ Chakra and section on *Working Through The Chakra*.) You are Here Now. That's the most important. When you become stronger, more in touch with yourself, more in touch with The Divine, you can revisit your past to correct the wrongs, to undo the spikes that pain you. Time is neither dead nor linear. Think of it as a hologram, your past, present and future all existing Now. Don't allow your analytical brain to come in right now to protest this idea. Give yourself a chance to *know* in a different way, in an intuitive way.

Don't focus on a huge project like being Enlightened or being freed from the Wheel of Samsara or whatever. It is a daunting task because it seems mammoth. Just focus on each single step you take. Focus on something you can grasp rather than something you cannot. Focus on You. It is that simple. There is nothing conceptual to begin with. You don't have to focus on something that is outside of yourself. Just focus on your breath. Focus on your body. It is there with you. There is no equipment to buy, no fancy clothes to wear, no club to join. There is also no excuse. The only cost you will incur is giving of your time. Won't happiness be worth a few minutes of your time each day? It is all down to you. If you are serious about wanting to be happy, you will make the time. Your body is the tool you have. Use it to discover your True Self. Use it to discover The Divine.

## As You Breathe, So You Become

There are many things you can live without in your life. There are even some parts of your body you can manage without and still live. People who have lost limbs or one of their five senses to disease or accidents are still capable of living a life. They may be challenged physically, emotionally and mentally but they can still live. But the one thing you cannot live without is your Breath. Your breathing sustains your physical life. This is so fundamental and so obvious to most people. Nobody can mistake the importance of breathing if we want to continue to live. And yet, it is very interesting that very few people pay attention to their breath nor place any importance on its quality and amount of intake.

Limited as it may be, let us use the analogy of breath as money.

We know that without money, there are many things we cannot buy, many things we cannot enjoy, there are places we cannot go. How we live our life, the type of food we eat, the kind of home we live in, the luxury of our leisure pursuits is entirely dependent on the amount of money we possess. (To keep our analogy simple, we won't go into the unique situation where we have no need of money whilst living in the convent, monastery or prison, etc.)

For the lay-person, the shortage or lack of money will certainly inhibit her life-style. Extreme lack of money means that we cannot even afford basic needs like food and shelter. Therefore it is possible that without money to buy or grow food, we could die. It is this understanding that motivates each and every one of us to work hard to earn money or to find a source of money through other means, like depending on a parent or spouse, government or charity, etc. We know that the quality of our life is dependent on the amount of money we can get hold of. To be without money is to be attacked by a financial virus, illness or disease – the comfort of our living is affected.

So we work, we save, we invest for our old age so that when we can no longer work, we have a pension which still pays for the things we need to live by. We have the added concern of making sure that there is enough money to pay our medical bills and perhaps a nursing home. We know that it is not a practical situation for the majority of us to start thinking about our pension when we are at our pensionable age; this process has to begin whilst we are still young and healthy, whilst we still can work and not when we are old. Let us look at our breathing in a similar vein.

Breathing is the currency of our life. Its quality determines the quality of your Vital Energy. The condition of your Vital Energy determines how you are, how you feel. Yet it is astonishing that we don't consider having to work hard to improve our breathing finances. We accept it as our natural right and we don't feel we need to do anything to improve its quality or its quantity. And yet we are astonished when we feel stressed or when illness or disease attacks us.

Every condition that you experience in your body, whether it is physical, emotional or mental can be traced back to the quality of your breathing or its lack. Amazing right? If you can comprehend this basic fact, then I am sure that you will re-think the way you treat your breath. Let us get re-acquainted with your Breath. Pretend you are meeting your long lost friend.

## Say Hello To Your Breath

Find yourself a quiet space. It does not have to be a quiet physical space. It can just be a quiet mental space. You can do this wherever you are, out in the woods, by the sea, on the downs, in a crowded bus or your office. If you think you are going to look weird with your eyes closed, just have them lowered. The idea of this is to shift your focus away from your physical eyes so that you won't be distracted by what you see. But if you find that you need to look at something, then so be it. Look at the tip of your nose, a flower or a lighted candle. You may notice that this simple action of lowering your eyes will create a slight shift in your mental make-up. Instead of seeing through your eyes, you may discover that your attention has automatically moved to that space between your eyebrows, the location of your Third Eye. If that has not happened, it's no big deal. It will eventually. But don't allow any exercise to create more tension in you. Inner bodywork is designed to help you release tension from your Mind and your Body, not add to it.

When an old friend you have not seen for a long time turns up at your house, what is the first thing you do? First you say Hello. Then you notice how she looks, how she has changed since you last met. You let her in through your front door of your house. It is the same with your Breath. Say a mental Hello to it because you have neglected to notice it for a long time. Let it in through the doors of your Body, i.e, through your nostrils. Notice how the Breath feels, how it touches the entrance of your nostrils, whether it is cool or warm. Can you feel its movement through your nasal passage? Is your Breath strong or weak?

There, that is a good start. It is that simple.

You don't need any special place or special time to do this. You can do this whilst waiting for someone, or are in a queue at the check-out, or in your car by a level crossing waiting for the train to pass by.

If you work closely with someone for a while or live with someone for some years, you will know the person's way of behaviour, idiosyncrasies and traits. You can tell her mood from the way the person is acting or reacting. This information can be useful to you, to avoid some nasty repercussion. In the same way, when you get to know your breath better, you can use this understanding to help you operate your life in a more efficient way and keep you at your optimum good health. So if you notice that you are taking your breath in small sips, it is telling you that your Mind is under tension and is expressing itself through your Body by tightening up the muscles of your jaw, your neck, your shoulders and elsewhere. All you need to do to remedy the situation is to stop taking small sips and breathe in a bit longer as though you are breathing in a smell that you like, the smell of woodlands fresh after the rain, lavender, roses or whatever. See if you can measure the length of your breath. Does it last 1-2-3-4 seconds or less? Urge it a little to last at least four mental counts as you Breathe IN and four counts as you Breathe OUT. One IN and one OUT is equal to One Round. Try ten. Then back to normal breathing.

Unless specified, all breathing exercises, both IN and OUT, should be done through the nose and not the mouth for two main reasons: 1) your nose has hairs to filter out unnecessary stuff the lungs do not need 2) your nose has minor Energy points or chakras which do influence your mental state.

(There are many yoga books with excellent breathing exercises. My own book, *Body And Mind Sculpture/Shape Up For Self-Discovery* has specific techniques for specific purposes. Do check the various books on various techniques if you want to improve your breathing. This book is focussed on the philosophical concept of breathing rather than a workbook of exercises.)

Physiologically, when you are breathing, you take in air that is a mixture of oxygen and other gases that will help your body to function efficiently. In humans, breathing is largely involuntary, i.e, breathing takes place regardless of whether you remember to do so or not. However, you can engage in voluntary breathing to influence your moods and your health since the level of breath is linked to the level of Pranic or Vital energy. Breathing properly helps you to improve your blood circulation and flush out the body's impurities through the lympathic system. Good energetic breathing will exercise your lungs and chest muscles, working the diaphragm, moving it up and down. As you are aware, your diaphragm is like a firm elastic arched underneath your breast-bone. When you breathe IN, this elastic move downwards so that your internal organs get a nice gentle massage and are bathed in the Vital Energy. When you breathe OUT, the elastic flexed upwards back into its arch, nudging the lungs into action, expelling the unneeded air. If you breathe shallowly, the effectiveness of this is lost. If you are not breathing IN deeply enough, the diaphragm has not got the opportunity to flatten against your abdominal organs to stimulate blood circulation. If you don't breathe OUT enough, the diaphragm does not have the energy to reach upwards enough to help your lungs expel the stale air that collects at the tip of your lungs. Of course other muscles and organs are involved as well. So, it is essential to remember that the ability to influence and control your breathing is the key to your health.

### Breathing – Your Medium To The Divine

Over and above the role of breathing in your physical health, breathing plays another very important role – that of being your medium to link up with The Divine. This is an Eastern way of thinking. If you are new to this idea, don't be alarmed. Just let yourself stay open. You don't have to rush into anything. The more you observe your breathing, the more you will see where it is taking you. Simply relax and enjoy.

The actual air we utilise when we breathe, oxygen, etc. exists in the physical realm. But in yogic philosophy, we are not just breathing in air but we are breathing in *prana*. We said in Chapter 1, that *prana* is usually translated as Life Force or Vital Energy. As we mentioned earlier, different cultures have different names for it. As Shakespeare said, *A rose by any name is still a rose*. The name is not crucial but the understanding is. *Prana* is more subtle than air. It exists in the *pranic* or Energy field. Just as the air we breathe travel through the trachea, bronchus and bronchioles to the lungs, *prana* travel through etheric pathways called *nadis* which exist in the subtle body. Altogether it is said that there are 72,000 *nadis*. In Sanskrit, the word, *nad* means movement or motion. Therefore a *nadi* means a *channel, stream or flow*. In yoga it is said that prana is the force which is responsible for the renewal of cells in the body. The more energised the cells are, the less susceptible are they to disease. If a person is well-charged with the pranic energy, the person can use the extra energy to heal others. Molecules vibrate at a slower pace at the physical level to create denser material like our body and all things physical. As the speed of the pace increases, we move into less dense dimensions. It is the breath that provides the bridge from our physical existence into the more subtle realms.

## Separateness and Oneness

When we view things from the perspective of our Ego-Self, we are separate bodies from other individuals, just as, for example, England is separate from France, two land masses that have their own geographical positions and identities. What separates the two countries is the English Channel, a wide body of water. More significantly, what separates the two nations are language, culture, attitude and a different way of looking at things. We can say the same for other countries, other nations separated from each other by sea or ocean. We establish this fact through empirical observation, i.e. using our physical eyes, in the same way that we can see that two human beings are two separate entities, not conjoined twins.

However, the development of analytical thought, advanced scientific methods and technology have given us a perspective that our human eyes alone could not give. For example, that the Earth is round and not flat, that the Earth rotates around the sun and not the other way round. The facts in themselves have not changed, which are, the Earth has always been spherical and that it rotates around the sun; only the methods of observation and comprehension have changed. Because our standpoint has changed, we are able to see the truer picture, the true reality.

This is exactly the same as our perception of The Divine Consciousness. The facts remain the same. The Divine is, and always has been present, it is a case of whether you have the standpoint to observe and note Her presence.

Let us return to our analogy of England and France. When we began to have the capacity to measure depths of the ground and ocean, we realise that the above separateness of islands, both huge and small, is actually only an aspect of the truth because the reality is that however great the distance is between land masses of countries, underneath it all, we are joined by the seabed, by the crust of the Earth. We are not really separate islands or countries floating above the land with no linkage to each other. In the same way, if we take a different perspective of people, then we can see that on another level, the spirit level, we are not separate beings because our consciousness will merge with other consciousness. It is the solidness of our Body which give rise to this idea of us being separate beings. That is why it's so important for us to make our spiritual connection for when we are connected to the Divine, our understanding of our fellow beings will also be changed and enhanced. True spirituality is not running away from mankind but is embracing mankind.

## Your *Chunnel* To The Divine Consciousness

When the Channel Tunnel was being constructed 40 feet under the seabed of the English Channel between England and France in the 1980s, people nicknamed it the *Chunnel*, a combination of the word *channel* and *tunnel*. If you permit me, I like to borrow the word *chunnel* (pronounced with its Gaelic lilt) to describe the link between us and The Divine Consciousness. Obviously, such an analogy is limited but it will provide the illustration for the point I am making here.

Work on the Channel Tunnel began simultaneously in England and France in December 1987. The portion under the seabed was to be the longest undersea tunnel in the world at 24 miles (39 km). Advanced laser technology guided the two tunnel boring machines (TBMs) towards each other. The British and French

TBMs broke through and met at the half-way mark under the seabed in December 1990. In December 1991, the two rail tunnels met at this same point. This engineering feat would have been impossible without modern technology, good planning and the right equipment.

In the same way, you need to create your *Chunnel* to The Divine Consciousness by boring deep within yourself. Imagine that you are on one side of the channel and The Divine is on the other, you need to start to make the link. (Remember that you have free will so no one can force you to do what you don't want to do.) Therefore you need to express the *desire* to know and understand The Divine. The moment you express this desire to want to know who you truly are and how The Divine is expressed, The Divine too will start digging from the other end (as such). You are never left on your own to wander around aimlessly, you will be guided by the laser technology of The Divine. Just as the engineers know that the two tunnels from England and France will eventually begin operation in 1994, you too will meet The Divine if you persevere in your spiritual practices and start operating your life with this connection intact.

Obviously, the existence of The Divine is not directly perceived in this world though its manifestations are there for you to see, e.g a beautiful rainbow, a gorge carved out in stone, the splendour of mountain ranges, etc. (I have a particular affinity with rainbows as I find them not only breathtakingly beautiful but also inspirational as it always lift my spirits to see one. When we discuss the seven gateways in our body to The Divine, you will again see the significance of the rainbow.) The awesome beauty of natural landscapes and creatures are signposts to us that The Divine is behind them all. But our world of matter operates on a grosser frequency than that inhabited by The Divine. The slower the movement of the atoms, the more gross the frequency is, creating solid matter. Therefore in order for us to be able to understand the Divine, we must of course get into the right frequency. Exactly the same as when you want to tune in to a particular radio station. If you want to listen to *The Archers* on Radio 4, it would be silly to tune in to Radio 2. Radio 4 is on FM 92.4 and no matter how much you press your ear to the radio, you will not get Radio 4 if you are on Radio 2's wave-length FM88.90.

This seems so obvious yet there are people who claim that The Divine does not exist. The trouble is that some people want to be able to verify the existence of The Divine easily. Sanskrit scholar A.T de Nicolas said in his work, *Avatara, "Some men refuse to recognise the depth of something because they demand that the profound should manifest itself in the same way as the superficial."* I have asked these disbelieving people if they have tuned into the right wave-length – i.e. through meditation and prayer and the answer is invariably "How can I pray when I don't believe there is a God?" And my response is. "How can you discover there is a God if you don't pray?" Prayer is a method of tuning in to the correct frequency. That is, if we really tune in; otherwise prayer can turn out to be an inner monologue – you telling The Divine what you want without listening to his answer!

All anyone needs to do to *know* the existence of The Divine is to fine-tune their frequency until you match the wave-length of The Divine. Simple really when you think about it. Only a fool will sit there by his radio and keep on tuning his radio to the wrong frequency and then grumble that he could not get Radio 4! And yet, so many people out there swear they know that The Divine does not exist when really they have not been on the right wave band at all!

This is not blind faith, someone telling you to believe without evidence and you have to believe blindly. At one point in our human history, we were not aware of Radio waves. Why? Because they were invisible and not easily detected. But radio waves have always been present, they are not new. What is new as that we have a means of detecting them through advanced technology. It is the same with your frequency to The Divine. It is there. You just need the 'technology' to get in tune with it. Our Spiritual Explorers provided you with various methods – through yoga, Tai Chi, Sufism, music, poetry, writing, meditation, chanting, etc. Test it for yourself. Fine-tune your own reception and you will get onto the correct frequency for you to communicate with The Divine. But the evidence must be perceived by yourself for you to know the truth. But I have to admit that it is not as easy as twiddling the knob on the radio though. I will admit to failing numerous times but we can get there in the end. What makes it difficult for us to get onto the correct wave-length to perceive The Divine is interference from the Mind, the interference being bad static to radio waves. The Mind produces doubts, rational arguments and confusing thoughts to prevent you from discovering the Truth. The Mind is part of the Ego-Personality or Operating Personality that is the individual and it is afraid to let go of its individuality as it fears to lose itself in the sea of Consciousness. The wonderful thing is that the moment you start to tune in, you become aware that you have been operating on a very low frequency all your life and thus have been identifying only with this body and this mind (the *sharira*). Soon as you manage to get into a different wave band, you will begin to notice different aspects of yourself and the world, what you thought were fixed boundaries of this mundane world suddenly become flexible and expansive. It is magical!

Many spiritual disciplines provide you with methods of fine-tuning your wave length. Different disciplines might use different words and fancy or cryptic terminology but ultimately the purpose is the same, to get you to refine the gross elements of this body and mind so that we begin to operate on a finer frequency that will enable us to comprehend The Divine. The process of refining our breath and our frequency has a marvellous side-effect, that of healing The Body, all the pain in your body, mind and heart, i.e, the *sharira*.

Of course, we have to start from where we are, with what we

have. We have this body, we have this mind. Your breath is the *chunnel*, the Channel Tunnel link to the subtler frequencies that exist and thereby to The Divine. The more you refine your breath, the more you refine your frequency. How easy can it get? The act of listening to your breath will begin from your physical ears but will lead into your inner ears. You are learning to locate (obviously *not* a physical location) and open them. There is not much point if, when you get onto the right frequency of your Radio station for you to then shut your ears. You won't be able to hear a thing! In the same way, if we managed to get onto the right frequency with The Divine, there's not a lot of good if we then can't hear! To be able to hear the subtler communication of The Divine, you need to open your Inner Ear. Just as we need to open our Inner Eye if we want to *see* in the subtler dimensions.

The Inner Ear is not that mystical. People who can *hear* a poetic rhythm when they hear words being recited or music already have this sense quite well-developed. It just needs to be more developed to hear The Divine. Human beings tend to focus on our five senses which deal with our outer world, but we forget that we really have other inner senses too to listen beyond the words someone is speaking, to see beyond the actions that someone is exhibiting. The process towards understanding The Divine is also a process of renewing our inner capabilities. That is why it appears that artistic and creative people have so-called visions more than people who are die-hard-analytical people. The latter disprove of things that are not hard facts and empirically testable facts so in the process, they lose the knack of sharpening their subtler tools of perception. More of this when we discuss the 5th and 6th gateways.

The constant bombardment of noise and a cacophony of sounds, bright lights, fast moving images like those on television and computers can deafen and dull us to our inner capabilities, make us forget that we even have them. And worse still. Where our inner ear and eye take us inwards, these disturbances tend to keep us focused on the outside. To escape from the outside to the inside is a difficult journey because the switch to the mind is too jarring, the mind cannot immediately relax. That is why hatha yoga is so helpful, using the body in action, putting it through the paces by executing postures to take you into gradual stillness. The transition is thus much more gradual and therefore is more likely to succeed in calming the body and mind rather than through grit force.

Get ready to be introduced to your Inner You.

---

**Something To Do (2):**

Take a walk today. If you are lucky enough to be able to get into the countryside, that is fantastic. But if not, even if you are in a city, you can do this exercise. Instead of blindly going about your usual activities, with your Mind in an accelerated gear of its own, try to be present. You are present when your Mind is engaged with your Body, with what you are doing. Notice something natural, for example, the sky, the grass. Really notice it. Not half-heartedly. See the colour, try to feel the texture, admire its beauty. Watch your feelings about it. You will find that as you do this, your breath will step into rhythm with you. This is a method of fine-tuning your frequency. The more your do this, the better you become at it.

---

## CHAPTER 3

# The Old View Of The Body

*"Self-love, my liege, is not so vile a sin as self-neglecting."*
William Shakespeare,
*King Henry V. Act ii. Sc. 4.*

Over the centuries, the body had been much maligned.

There have been and still are religious sects that treat the body as an object of sin and evil, the habitat of Original Sin. It follows therefore that the body has to be starved, whipped and scourged. Some early believers wore hair-shirts and flogged themselves with cat-of-nine-tails. Did they do this to drive the devil out of themselves or did they do this because their body evoked sensual appetites which they felt took them away from God? Whatever their motivation was, there had to be an element of revulsion over the body and fear about the body, perhaps fear of not being able to control the body's appetites. For those who believe in a benevolent God who had supplied them with a body, the abhorrence of the body does not make sense. It is incongruous to love a God yet not love his gift.

If the body is a temple of God, how can it be vile? Why should the body be treated with such a base irreverence? Such attitudes drive a wedge in the populace, those who indulge and those who abstain. The ones who indulge in the emotions and feelings generated by the body feel guilty; the ones who abstain feel deprived and repressed with both running to Confession every time they indulge in their senses. Neither feels good about himself. This is indeed a sorry state.

No true religion can be based on fear, either of the body or of being punished by a God. Fear takes you away from The Divine not towards it. Anything to be feared is a captor who has an undesirable hold over you. Your connection to The Divine is based on your freedom of choice and to live with joy.

## Don't Deny Your Body

As a famous popular song says, "Let us start at the very beginning...." Before we strive for a huge goal like being enlightened, let us start at the beginning with what we are. We are a Physical Body. There is no doubt about this. Even if we want to be very philosophical and claim that we are a Spirit having a physical existence, what we cannot deny is that we do own and live in a physical body. Yes, your physical body is a vehicle for your Soul but it is still made of matter. The concept of Soul and Spirit is harder to comprehend but a physical thing like our body is easy for us to handle and to know. To deny the fact of our physicality would be ridiculous.

Why deny the body? Let us have a better understanding so that we can enjoy our body without making the enjoyment sinful. What would be the use of God providing us with senses if we are to deny all of them? What we need is perspective – perspective to know how not to overindulge our senses to the detriment of our Body, Mind and Spirit.

So why not start with what we have – to discover what we may not have yet?

## Experiencing The World Through Your Senses

Even if you don't believe in an afterlife or worse, a purpose to your physical life, you can at least accept the idea that whilst you are on this earth, you will **experience**. So why not make that experience an interesting and good one? You will be surprised how much the quality of that experience is down to you. Whatever happens, the real experience of a situation is down to how you respond to that experience.

You cannot experience without the body, without your senses.

If you are lucky, you have all of your five senses intact: To smell, taste, see, feel and hear. Of course you know what they are but you need to be reminded that they are given to us by The Divine so that we can appreciate the world better. If we believe in a good God who created the world, then surely we must enjoy God's creations and admire the sky, the clouds, the trees, the meadows and rivers and everything of this earth. Surely it will be a sin not to. From having done your exercise in the Something To Do (2) section, you will know that focusing your senses on things of nature, admiring the works and manifestations of The Divine, could lead to your connection with The Divine. Don't ever lose the sense of wonder. When you gasp with joy at the beauty of a rainbow, the rays coming down through the clouds, the full-moon against a velvet sky or the sight of a newborn babe, you are celebrating the qualities of The Divine. You can't be wrong.

But it can go wrong when over-focusing on the senses lead you to an over-indulgence whereby we become too attached to them and lose touch with the idea of what they are for. The senses help us to experience the world, to admire what The Divine has created so that we can be linked to The Divine. It is when we lose this connection with The Divine that we lose touch with reality and become attached to the unreal, the pseudo world of emotions, mind and intellect. We are reduced to our sense-experience in itself so that it becomes an end in itself without using it as a trajectory to discover The Divine. This suggests that the balance is lost. We will discuss more on the senses in a later chapter to show you how you can use your senses as gateways or portals into the Energy world because the senses are the expression of the seven major Energy Centres or chakras that are located in your *Pranic* body.

## Our Current Preoccupation With The Body

It would appear that our current preoccupation with the beauty of the body is an act of extreme love of the body. But in truth, our current obsessive view of the body is in fact a dislike or worse, a hatred, for what the body truly is. We put a lot of emphasis on the body, we spend millions of dollars and pounds on it, dressing it, indulging it but we do not love it. To love someone or something is to allow that someone or something be what it is in its true essence. We cannot say we love somebody if we manipulate and force the person to behave in the way we expect the person to behave. True love is letting go of your expectations of that person. In the same way, we cannot love our body if we cannot allow our body to take its true course of nature and we have to manipulate and force it to conform to our ideals of what a body should look like. This is not love, it is possession. Possession of someone or something is coupled with the fear of that someone or something changing.

Letting our body take its true course of nature does not mean neglecting it. It still necessitates our looking after it but not forcing it by bending it to our will in order that we may achieve or maintain a certain image. Each of our bodies has its own structural bony framework in the skeleton which supports and protects our vital organs. Like the structure of a building, this skeletal structure can support a reasonable band of weight. Not one weight but a *band* of weight. This is important to understand because it will help you *not* to be fixated with a specific weight for yourself. A band of weight between such-and-such where the weight is evenly distributed along the structure you were born with. Soon as the weight is beyond what the structure can support or if the weigh is unevenly distributed, the framework experiences stress. The weight of your organs do not change. When you put on weight what changes is the weight of the muscles and additional fat. The extra weight of muscle is not necessarily detrimental as we can see from athletes and particularly weight-lifters who use their body-weight for a specific purpose. What is detrimental for the body is excess fat that puts unnecessary weight on the organs and structures of the body and obstructs its natural functioning. This is logical. Thus there is an optimum weight for a particular structure.

In the body, this optimum weight is suggested by the size of our bones, organs, our muscles and soft tissues and the work they must do to activate our everyday activities; for example a working farmer would need more developed muscles than a person working in a sedentary job thus he can afford to weigh more than the office worker. Therefore when we idealised a particular shape or size, like Size Zero, we are working against the natural stance of our body. We are expecting everyone to conform to one shape and size which is so ridiculous. Yet our fashion magazines extol this kind of body manipulation. A few people in power set this image as the ideal image and we unwittingly follow. A few people in power set the perfect female body as being thin with big breasts; a perfect male body as one with muscles, washboard tummy and a tight bottom. Then we get inundated with images of idealised bodies, not realising the true picture that the owners of those bodies have to starve themselves – and the result of that is that they feel ill, get very ratty and are basically unhappy people. Why do you think that famous models have anger-management problems? It is not just about their ego. It is about the lack of happiness in themselves. Of course there are underweight people who don't have to starve themselves. However, when we look at the so-called beautiful images on a cat-walk, screen or glossy magazine, you must remember that all you are seeing is their outside shells not their inside condition. (Plus the fact that many images in magazines tend to be air-brushed for effect.) But the repetition of such images that we see everywhere act like a kind of drug, making us soporific and is responsible for us losing our innate intuition and we then began to accept this as the norm for beauty. This is what advertising does. We are being manipulated and we unwittingly allow ourselves to be manipulated. It is time to break out from your drowsiness, be yourself and support the Real You. It is time for you to look beyond the physicality of you.

Neither being Size Zero or grossly overweight is being kind to the body. If you are very underweight, your body system cannot support the natural functioning of various organs so you get headaches, tire easily, you lack strength and stamina, you let in viruses to affect your body, which in turn makes you irritable and you have difficulty coping with the simple challenges of life. You might even develop phobias of all sorts. But if you overindulge on wrongful foods and become grossly over-weight or you don't exercise, you are putting stress on you body's system. A constantly over-loaded vehicle will mean undue stress on the suspension and over time that suspension will break. Just as in the body. An over-weight body puts pressure on the heart, the knees, hips, kidneys, on the blood running smoothly through your circulatory system. It is not coincidental that generally, people who have had hip replacements or knee and heart problems tend to not exercise or are overweight. So weight control is not about vanity but is about the optimum weight a framework can carry for it to function efficiently in its chosen activities and to keep it healthy. Once you have this clearly in your mind, you can stop others from inflicting on you what your ideal body weight should be. You gain a better perspective but you also start to be responsible for your body, keeping it as healthy as it can possibly be till it is time to trade it in.

(On this score I would like to make a relevant point that some New Age type of books seem to ignore – the body is built to last only a finite time. No matter how spiritual you become, the body will still have to degenerate and die. This is inescapable. Otherwise all the Enlightened Sages, our Spiritual Explorers, would still be alive! This follows that at some point or other, the body will be attacked by some disease or other which will take us to our body's natural death. Therefore I feel that some New Age teachers tend to over-simplify things when they imply that our level of spiritual advancement is correlated to the degree of our health. Also, the facile attribution of certain conditions of parts of the body and certain diseases to the attitude of the sufferer can be damaging. I believe that pointing fingers is not helpful. However I do agree that it is correct to say that each person suffering has to look at what the condition, disease or infliction is *teaching* them and to rise above their physical condition. But to state categorically that everything that had befallen a person is brought on by themselves is far too sweeping. I think it is more complicated than that. And I don't know the answer.)

## Fear of annihilation

To not allow our body to be natural is to not love it. We hook in to the collective fear of not being accepted and adulated, of being an outsider, of being old. We suck out fat from our bodies, we cut and stitch our faces, we plump up our lips, we inject poison into our foreheads so that we can remain youthful as if old age is a disease. Somehow along the way, we have lost our balance and our perspective. Instead of viewing the body as only one part of ourselves, as a vehicle for our spirit, we have begun to see our body as the whole or as the only thing that matters. We have come to identify ourselves totally as the body and worse, we also look upon other bodies and identify them as our family, friend or foe. This false identification is the reason for our fear. Firstly, we make this erroneous identification with regard to ourselves; and secondly to others. This is the kind of identification that leads to warfare.

It is inevitable that the body must degenerate and then must die. *Dust Thou art and to dust Thou shalt return.* The Catholics are reminded of this on Ash Wednesday. But it should be *to dust Thine body shalt return.* Somehow the *thou,* the Self, has been mistaken to be just the body! The True You never dies. You are more than the body. As soon as we become aware of this, the fear dissipates. Because what we fear is an annihilation of the self. But what really happens is that physical death is an annihilation of a particular physical body, but never the Real Self.

When people say they need to have plastic surgery to feel more confident about themselves, these people are identifying themselves with their body. This is identification with the external form. If they need surgical intervention to correct a condition like incontinence or a face scarred by fire or an accident which distresses them, then it is perfectly acceptable. Surgery will help such people to feel more confident to go out. But if a person can only feel confident because the shape of her nose or breasts, to her mind, is wrong then plastic surgery is never going to give her true confidence. She needs divine surgical intervention with her mind! For in focusing on one part of the body, it is the body which has come to be of such importance until it determines her sense of identity.

When you attach yourself to the imbalanced idea of the body's importance, you develop a love-hate relationship with it. You over-indulge the body through excessive food or sex then you hate it and punish it through extreme starvation and sick sex (or something to the effect). This wrongful identification is an error which is the cause of fear and most of our suffering. Of course you will live in fear of your body degenerating if you believe that the body is the total You. But if you can realise that the total You is not just the body, then that fear will dissipate. It is a costume you wear for this part you are taking, in this life-time, as I have taken the costume of *Phine* for this particular life. When the run for this play (this physical life-time) is over, I give up my costume (my body) to find another more appropriate costume for the next character I am to play. The Real Me, who is a conglomerate of all the parts I have played, and will play, does not die. So what is there to fear?

You don't have to believe in this in the sense of blind faith and accepting what I say. Find it out yourself. This knowledge is yours to know when you start to operate on a subtler dimension. By honing your skills to navigate in the subtler realms, you will become aware that your Real Self is the driver of the vehicle of the

47

body and is not the body itself.

## Functionality Is Not Life

These days, there is a GPS system like the *Tom-Tom, Charmin*, etc. that you can fit into your car and it can tell you with a human voice how to get to a place, where the best hotel is, where to eat, what to see. It can give you second-by-second instructions on where and when to turn, which direction to take and even to slow down when you go pass the speed limit and where the camera is! We are aware that without someone working the computer and setting the commands the car cannot operate on its own. We know that neither the *Tom-Tom* nor the car is the driver. It will be silly for us to identify the car as ourselves. Yet we do that with our body and mind. Our body and particularly our mind have been operating on a kind of Blue-Tooth technology, both can largely work almost independently of us. Hence it makes it easy for us to lose sight of the fact that there used to be a Higher Self (our Real Self) who governs both our body and mind. However efficient or intelligent the vehicle is, the programme at the onset must still be installed by a human being. It's the same if we could build a human-looking robot that carries out what looks like human functions. The car manufacturers *Honda* in Japan have built a humanoid robot called *Asimo* who can speak, walk and perform simple tasks like serving coffee, etc. But we must not mistake *functionality* with *life*. Both the vehicle and robot can function but it does not have a life of its own. In the same way, your Body and Mind do not have a life of its own without You.

That is why all spiritual disciplines help you to become aware of how you have ceded control to the mechanical body and mechanical mind. Knowing this will help you to resume control of your vehicle and for you to get back into the driving seat. That is why spiritual disciplines *are necessary* for each and every one of us and not just for those who are interested or the chosen few. Spiritual practices are not confined to any particular religion, theistic beliefs or theistic icons. Spiritual disciplines are not designed to be hocus-pocus techniques that allow you to see fairies, angels, spirit guides or colourful auras or take you to Atlantis or Heaven. (However, part of the change that occurs in yourself on a spiritual journey could enable you to develop your sixth sense to such a degree that you can indeed view these things but this is not the goal. In yoga these are called *siddhis* which we are warned not to allow to side-track us from our ultimate spiritual goal. We will discuss this further in Chapter 11, the section on *Intuition – The Sixth Sense.*) Spiritual techniques were designed by our Past Spiritual Explorers to clear away the cobwebs that blind you to Reality. The different techniques in different spiritual disciplines give you different routes to help you to recapture your ability to see yourselves as you truly are. You are pulsating with Aliveness and you are better aware of your more subtle body of Energy. Once you know who you truly are, you will not fall into the trap of identifying only with your body (or mind). This is thus a liberation from your old idea of Self and thereby from the fears and pain that bind you to that old idea of Self. With your liberation comes enlightenment. That is why Enlightenment is not a far-off goal in some Never-Neverland. It can occur here and now, when you brush off the dust of ignorance that blinds you thus allowing your Soul Light to shine.

So pick up your metaphorical sword and lash at your ignorance. There is a lovely symbol in Tibetan Buddhism which represents this idea in the form of a Deity called Manjushri. He is often depicted in all his splendour, sitting on a thousand-petaled lotus, the sword raised in his right hand, the book of True Knowledge on his left. He uses the sword to cut away the ignorance and the ties that bind. That is why he has often been used in schools and educational institutions as their symbol and mentor. (As a matter of clarification, although the pronoun *He* is used in describing Manjushri, the deity is really genderless and some people use the pronoun *She*. In many paintings and

49

pictures, Manjushri is depicted with a feminine face and a bare torso which curved like that of a woman rather than that of the shape of a man.)

## Neglect Is As Vile

Gautama Buddha himself tried starvation and total disregard for the body as a means to Enlightenment. He deprived his body of food and exercise and sat and sat for days, weeks and months. Such deprivation have resulted in hallucinations for some ascetics. But after his long sojourn Gautama realised that this was not the way. The body is the vehicle for the spirit and thus has to be treated with respect. Without a physical form, the spirit cannot express itself. So, just as over-indulgence of the body is wrong, so too is neglect of it.

There is no mileage in either rejecting the body or ignoring it. Your body has to last you the lifetime you need to do your work here on this earth. Therefore it makes good sense to take care of it as you must take care of your car if you want your car to take you safely on your travels. You MOT it, you send it to be serviced, you ensure that you put in the right fuel and at the right time. If you neglect to take fundamental care of the car, it will not perform with the efficiency you require it to. So don't you think it is arrogant to expect the body to perform to its optimum best when you do not care for it? As the saying goes, self-love may be vile but not as vile as self-neglect.

If you poison the body's system with bad food, you will be unhealthy. It's quite straightforward really. It does not require a sage to arrive at this observation. If you don't exercise the muscles, they atrophy. Joints have their various range of movement which we rarely utilise in our daily life so joints become squeaky, arthritic or stiff. You don't necessarily have to go to a gym but you need to either walk, run, swim or do something physical sometime each week to keep your body in good order. Laxed muscles are not only unattractive, they cannot perform their best when they are not toned. Think of your tummy muscles: an apron of fat and muscles support all your internal organs. If you have a belly that jiggles when you move, try to imagine what is happening to the organs inside you and what it is doing to your spine. The organs won't exactly get displaced but they would not keep to their correct positions comfortably. And of course, if things are not in their correct places then ill health results. Your tummy muscles also form the other half of the muscular corset which supports your back muscles. If you are in bad shape in front, it is likely that you are in bad shape at the back. Think of a boat with its mast and riggings. Your backbone is the mast. When your riggings, i.e. front and back muscles and ligaments are not as taut as they should be, the mast loses its capacity to remain upright. Your structural framework is held up and kept in its rightful place by your ligaments and muscles. Lose the tone in this and you will lose the integrity of your posture. And though it sounds very basic, poor posture is the root of many bodily evils and diseases. Poor posture can result in the curvature of your spine. Any deviation of the spine from its comfortable and natural stance is bad for the spinal cord and nerves and plays havoc with the body and its health. The vertebrae of your spine are bony and strong because they need to protect your body's important soft tissue, your body's main communication channel, the spinal cord. Spinal nerves run from your spinal cord to every part of your body, sending signals from the brain. Any damage to your spinal cord damages the part of the body it feeds. So caring for your body is not a sin, neglect is. (Later on, I will explain why the spine is so important in yoga and why many of the yogic postures help to improve the health of the spine.)

## What It Means To Be Present

The simple act of paying attention to your posture is a call for you to notice where you are at. This is a call for you, the Real You, to be present here and now. For you to know who you really are, you need to be present, not far away. For example if you want to know your children, you have to spend quite a lot of time with them. If you are always away from them they start growing and very quickly, you have lost their childhood. So if you want to know them, you try not to travel too far away from them or for prolonged times. It is the same with yourself. If You want to know who you truly are, come back from wherever you have been travelling. We do this travelling in many ways, mostly through our mind which is what we will be discussing in the next chapter. So be here. Be present. Just be. That is an essential aspect of your *be-ing*.

So when you do the simple act of paying attention to your posture, you are be-ing. You are here. This is a fundamental aspect of yoga. Union. United. In Hatha Yoga, when you execute a posture, you should be-ing. Be in your body, united with your breath. Not somewhere else. If you are thinking of how well you look in your leotards or designer yoga outfit, how well you are executing your posture, yesterday's film, tomorrow's dinner, etc., you are somewhere else, not in your body. That is why what is showing outside is not the true aspect of yoga, what is taking place inside is what counts.

Although attention to your body is physical, it is the starting point to connect with your Spirit and to The Divine Consciousness. The Bible says *Be still and Know that I am God.* It suggests that if you are not still and you are gadding about, it is harder for you to get to know God. If you take away the words, *that I am God*, you are left with the words, *Be still and know*. This is telling you that to *know,* not in the intellectual way but in the intuitive way, to comprehend The Divine, you need to *be still*. Take away the words, *still and know* and you are left with just the words *Be*. It's a small word with a big concept!

The whole art of most spiritual practices is learning how to just *be.*

When you *be*, you are free from the form that you took (i.e. your body and mind), you are free from concepts, you are free from the rules, conditions and social mores that the Operating Personality is subjected to. When you *be*, you enter into a special space.

The journey in this book is to help you to remember who you really are. Not through mystical processes but through paying attention to your Body and your Mind and understanding how both can influence you into forgetfulness of your True Nature and of The Divine. It is that simple. The wonderful thing is that you are in charge of the process, no one else. You don't have to believe. All you have to do is practise. *Begin at the beginning*, as we said earlier. Begin with yourself. You will regain your rightful inheritance and re-discover the capacity for joy and everlasting happiness.

---

### Something To Do (3):

Do yourself a favour, throw away your weighing scales.

Judge your health not by your weight alone. Judge it on how far you can walk without gasping, without your knees screaming. Judge it by how well you feel each morning, how you do and tackle things each day. Judge your emotional and mental health by the words you use to others – and to yourself. Be kind to yourself too. You can't be in the same state of physical health you were ten or twenty years ago. Be realistic. Help yourself to improve but don't murder your joy in the process.

---

## CHAPTER 4

# Effect Of The Mind On The Body

*"For fickle is the mind, impetuous, exceeding strong: how difficult to curb it! As difficult as to curb the wind"*
Bhagavad Gita, Chapter 6, Verse 34

I have not enlarged on the influence of the mind on health initially so that you had time to be reacquainted with your body first. But really, the mind is far more influential on your health than even the body. The World Health Organisation defined good health as being healthy in *both* body and mind. Modern psychological studies reveal what the yogis know for millennium – that whatever is happening in our mind is translated in the body. If your mind is fearful, thinking of negative things happening to you, negative events interfering with your life, then you find that you seem to be beset with physical problems, like poor breathing, headaches, pain in your joints, easily susceptible to colds, fevers, etc. Our mind activates the brain and the brain reacts according to the stimulant it receives from the mind. Then the brain triggers hormones to be released into the body thus influencing the state of the body.

So if you take a nice gentle walk in the woods, your body is getting good fresh air and your brain is releasing endorphins into the blood. That is why you feel good after a walk or an exercise session like yoga. Endorphines are your feel-good hormones. But if you are agitated on your walk, your brain thinking of work or family problems then your brain releases adrenaline into the blood stream. You won't be feeling relaxed after this sort of walk. An overload of adrenaline makes your heart beat faster, keeps your blood pressure high, draws the blood away from the digestive system. This hyper-state is necessary if you are about to shoot a Class 5 rapids or jump out of an aeroplane or hunt a tiger. But if you were only going to flop onto a comfy sofa to watch television, then the excess adrenaline has nowhere to go because it does not get utilised. Prolonged surges of adrenaline affect your body and its organs in negative ways thus leading you on a downward spiral in relation to good health. Think of excessive adrenaline like a hyperactive child with no parental control, it runs amok and wreaks havoc all over the place.

You will find that when you are stressed, upset or ill, the thing that receives your total attention is how your body feels, how your mind feels, how you feel. This means that you are pulled down to the level of the *sharira*, The Body. Although the initial attention to your body is helpful for you to get to know your body, too much attention means a wrong kind of focus. If any part of your body, heart and mind is caught in pain, you are in a state of unease or *dis*-ease. That is why it is hard to be generous, warm and pleasing to others when you yourself are in any kind of pain or undergoing any suffering. It is also impossible to focus your mind on The Divinity when you are in this state. (Except perhaps to rail at Her for letting you become ill!) If you feel that you have any contribution to make to this world or this planet, start by working on yourself; to make a difference to the world, you need to free yourself from your own suffering and pain first – to escape the shadow you have fallen under.

## Dispel the shadows

For many thousands of years, the yogis have already been aware of the shadow we cast upon ourselves. When you are in shadow, you are cut off from the Divine Light. So the Early Spiritual Explorers gave us routes and methods whereby we can reconnect with the Divine to bring Light into our life. Hence they have devised exercises, both physical and meditative to rid yourself of the problem at the root – i.e. the mind. Yoga, like Buddhism, is above all, a system of psychology which assists you in under-standing what your Mind is doing and then how to take control of it.

But as the above quote says, the mind is *"as difficult to curb as the wind"*!

So I was being a mite facetious when I remarked that it was easy to connect to The Divine. It is and it isn't. This is one of the reasons for writing this book. I used to be frustrated as a new Seeker when every self-help book tells you how easy it is to *clear your* mind or to be enlightened. Many of them give the impression that if you follow such and such a plan, hey presto! Your mind will be peaceful and calm and you will be enlightened. I wanted a book which tells of some attainment but also the struggles- in other words, a more realistic path that has relevance in day to day living on this planet Earth. I want to show that an ordinary person like me, even if I am nowhere near being an Enlightened Being, can reap huge rewards from daily spiritual practices – even if one spends a meagre ten minutes at it each day to begin with, simply by becoming aware – first of your breath. I am confident that once you begin taking this small first step, the rest of the journey will happen because you will have glimmers of insight that will encourage you to want to discover more. You will be motivated, not from fear but from a sense of wonder of the whole internal vista that presents itself to you.

### Identifying With The Mind

The breath is indeed the conduit to go from our grosser frequencies into the more subtle realms. But the problem lies in the fact that our Mind has become a soft-gloved dictator, leading us where we don't want to go. The Mind tells us what to do, how to feel, how to react. We are so in step with the Mind that we lose the capability of separating ourselves from it. So if I am thinking "Nobody likes me because I am fat and black," and I take this thought to be the Real me, then I suffer. It is actually the Mind who is thinking that thought. The thought pertains to my physical appearance, not my Real Self. (People in Singapore translate the Chinese or Malay concept of *brown* or *tanned* into *black* when they speak English. So my bete noir (pardon the pun) has been my complexion. Instead of being called *brown,* I was called *black* all the years I was growing up. As this was a pejorative term in the Far East, I came to consider myself ugly.) The latter is the kind of identification that is inaccurate, an identification that stemmed from other people's view of you. I had limited myself by identifying myself with other people's words and my Mind. I took the thought to be the same as the one observing the thought. Like our analogy in Chapter 1, of the car not being the driver, we have to pull ourselves away from the Mind to come to the realisation that the totality of who we are is not the Mind. In the same way that we identify wrongfully with our body as being the Real Me and causing us to be unhappy, identifying with the mind is also wrongful identification – bringing us suffering and pain. But the moment You, the Real Self is *present,* the duplicity of the Mind is found out, like finding out that someone has played a trick on you. The moment this happens, the Real You becomes an observer, observing what is taking place in the mind and in your body. I (the Real I) can then *look* at my body and my mind and say "Okay, so my body is brown and a bit over-weight. My mind is having a problem with that. *I don't.*" You have extricated yourself because you have taken back the power from the Mind. You are back in the driving seat.

To help you to extricate yourself from your mind, to help you to understand that your mind and You are not the same, don't suppress or deny any experience. Watch your thought, watch your emotions. Once again, observe your breath. Notice for yourself what happens to your breath when you are feeling anxious or pressured, when you are not sure of yourself. Notice what happens when you are running for the bus or when you are angry. Is your chest tight, your breathing short? Or is it flowing nicely and long? I'm sure you will note that the moment things go wrong in your life, you are so concentrated on everything that upsets you that your breath becomes short and unstable. When you ration your breath, your body goes into a state of red alert, muscles become tensed, your internal organs are tensed, your mind is tensed. As you well know, when you make decisions in this hyper tensed condition, they are usually not the best ones. This is because you become too engrossed in your body, in matter. You start to lose the connection with your Higher Self, the part of you that is relaxed and possessed intuitive knowledge. And worse, you lose the connection with The Divine – because your *chunnel* becomes blocked. There is a huge tract of obstructions between you and the Divine.

## Jump-Start Your Spiritual Batteries

That is why all spiritual disciplines, both Western and Eastern, have devised a quick remedy to enable you to re-connect back to The Divine quickly. The quick-cure will help you to lose any tension you have in your Body as rapidly as possible and to get the breath to flow unimpeded. It is a jump-start to your spiritual batteries, just like when you have to do so when your car is reluctant to move.

You jump-start your batteries by **lengthening your breath**. It's very simple. Something you can do anywhere and any time; no equipment needed, no teacher needed. Notice where your breath is, then just stretch your breath to a mental count of 4 or 6 or 8. Keep to the same length for three rounds. One In and One Out is considered One Round. Take a rest between each round. (Unless advised, in general yogic breathing, the breath is always taken through the nose and out through the nose. There are minor Energy Points or chakras in the nose that are triggered off by the breathing process.) The immediate effect will be that your heartbeat slows down, your blood pressure comes down and your muscles start to relax. If you find this very difficult to execute on your own, carry a CD in your car or an MP3 player with a breathing exercise on it, or relaxing music that can help you to achieve this condition. (We will talk about the beneficial effects of chanting in Chapter 13 – *Sound & Mantra*)

The moment you do this, taking over the breathing pattern which has largely become involuntary, you are starting to take the reins of control back from your Dictator Mind. You are back in the driving seat. You are Present in the Now. You, the Real You, is present when your mind is not scuttling off somewhere, like at yesterday's conversation with your friend, last year's quarrel with your partner, tomorrow's situation with your finances, this evening's arrangement about dinner, etc. The Present is Now, not yesterday, not tomorrow, not afterwards. The link with your breath is in the Now. Understanding this, let us look at what is obstructing our true knowledge of who we are.

For you to uncover who you really are, you also need to do some spring-cleaning.

## Clean Up Your Lampshades

We are so convinced that we are this body and this mind because we can see and touch solid matter. For a moment suspend your belief. (You don't have to suspend your belief after you have access to the knowledge intuitively.) Step outside yourself for this exercise so that you are looking down upon yourself. Of course I mean this figuratively so if it helps you, close your eyes after reading all this and try to see yourself from outside.

See a light bulb shining brightly. This is your Soul, Your Spiritual Light manifested in your being. (Just for clarification for those who are unsure of some spiritual semantics: a Soul is one particular incarnation or manifestation of the Spirit. So when we talk about Spirit, we are talking about that part of you which is beyond your individual Soul, the part that has a pervasive capacity to connect with other Spiritual Consciousness and The

Divine Light. Your Soul remains in this particular body of yours so that when your Soul leaves, your body dies. This is my understanding anyway at this point in time and I am prepared to be challenged.)

Liken your Soul Light to a lighted bulb on a lamp in your home. More than not, you will place a shade over the bulb. You will probably agree that the amount of light that is let through into your room is dependent on the wattage of the bulb plus the density of the material used in making the lamp-shade. Of course the wattage and material you choose depends on the atmosphere you want to create in that particular room. But for our analogy, we will view the lampshade as obstructing the light coming through.

Let us, for argument sake to simplify matters, say that as a Soul, our wattage is the same as all other Souls. In yogic philosophy, our Soul Light Bulb is covered by not one lampshade but five! Naturally, this is figuratively speaking  as they are not really lampshades but sheaths or envelopes (sometimes called *bodies*) that are denser than the Light. In Sanskrit, each sheath or envelope is called a *kosha*. The word itself is not that important, but the understanding is. As a reminder, in yogic philosophy, the percentage of density of a material is dependent on the vibrational index of the molecules holding them together, the slower the vibration, the denser the material, the faster the vibration, the less dense it becomes.

As you know if you put one lampshade over a lighted bulb, it will diminish the light from the bulb just that little bit. But if you used four, that light will be diminished considerably. How much light is still shining through depends on the type of material you used for the shade, silk or velvet will make a huge difference, plus whether the lampshade is clean or dusty. The whole process of Spiritual discipline is thus to clean up your lampshade so that your Soul Light can shine through and inclusive in this process is that of making your Spirit connect to The Divine Spirit. It is like in the fable about Aladdin's Lamp, rub the lamp till it is clean, then the genie will come out. So rub or clean your lampshade so that the genie in you, your Soul Light can shine forth lighting up your life and the world. If you recall the story of *Aladdin*, the genie has the power to grant wishes. The genie that you release is your own Soul Power and you can grant yourself your wishes! This is the power of manifestation. This becomes possible because you have linked up with The Divine Energy where you become super-charged so your thought-wish will attract what you wish for. But don't be intoxicated by your new-found power to manifest. Be very careful of what you wish!

## Your Lampshades

All analogies are limited so it is the same with lampshades. But they can be useful in a limited way to illustrate a point. Lampshades are in our material world and therefore they have clear boundaries. In the case of the *kosha*, they are inter-dimensional so they have no solid boundaries nor are they visible in the empirical sense. If your analytical brain rejects this idea violently, don't despair but do allow yourself time and space to key into your intuition to perceive the idea so that you can work with it for a while.

Starting from the densest *kosha* or sheath and working inwards, the body is the First Sheath, called the *Annamaya Kosha* or *Food Sheath*. (No. 1) Remember that if the Sanskrit term is a hindrance, ignore it. You can relate it to it as a number as in One, or use the English equivalent. Just be aware that as the sheaths go inwards, its density decreases until it reaches the Soul Light. Bear in mind also that the word *inwards* is a directional word to give us some reference point. In actuality the inner sheaths are not heavy and dense as the body therefore it has a capacity to permeate outside of the heavier denser material of the body and filter into each other. So for instance if you stand outside of yourself and look down on yourself, the inner sheaths could be seen as being *in* as well as *outside* of the body. If you can be viewed as a hologram then the various layers/sheaths would permeate out from the centre where the Soul Light is. I think this is why in Celtic spirituality, the body is said to be *in the Soul* because the Soul is not limited by the body and is expansive thus making the body a smaller and more limited item. The Food Sheath is the level where we are trapped if we identify ourselves solely as our body. It is called the Food Sheath for the obvious reason that we feed it physical food. In yoga, the air we breathe is also considered as food.

The second Sheath is called the *Pranamaya Kosha* or *Energy Sheath* (No. 2). This is the level of your Vital or Life Force. Acupuncture, acupressure and many of the Eastern massage techniques and Eastern exercises like hatha yoga, tai chi, Reiki etc. works on this level. In Western mysticism, this is considered to be the Etheric Body. Acupuncture, for instance, uses needles to stimulate the Energy Points or Nodes to stimulate the chi or *prana* to flow unimpeded. Disease occurs when this Vital Energy is not feeding a particular part of the body. We will return to this further when we discuss the seven Energy Portals. You tend to be a Heart Person when you operate from this level, focusing on your feelings and emotions.

The third is *Manomaya Kosha* or Mental Sheath (No. 3). This is the level of the mind and can be divided into the instinctive mind, intellect and memory. Just to make it clear, instincts refer to the innate reaction like that of an animal. It does not require thinking, it just happens, like a knee-jerk reaction. The instinctive mind serves its purpose by protecting us from danger, making sure we eat, making sure we breathe and all the basic needs for us to live as an organism. The basic need to have sex and procreate falls under this umbrella. The intellect reasons by helping us to make sense of our experiences and to interpret them and to help us get into appropriate action. For example, if we encounter a grizzly bear, our instinct might be to run, but our intellect might remind us that the grizzly is short-sighted and would be more alert if it sensed movement and interpret it as danger so our intellect might advise us to stand still till the grizzly goes away. Our storehouse of memories also comes under this umbrella so sometimes our reaction to something could be a result of a memory. For example, if we react with an unwarranted fear when we see a dog, it could be that we had been bitten by one when we were a child. You are operating at this level if you are very much a Head Person, using your mind most of the time. In Western mysticism, this is the level of the Lower Astral Body.

No. 4 is the *Vijnanamaya Kosha* or Intuitive Knowing Sheath. Sometimes *Vijnana* has been translated as *Knowledge* and thus this sheath has been called the *Knowledge Sheath*. I feel that in the West we often view knowledge as Intellectual Knowledge and since it is not so for this sheath, calling it an *Intuitive Knowing* is more appropriate. As intuition leads to wisdom or comes from wisdom, hence this sheath has also been called a *Wisdom Sheath*. If and when we arrive at this level, we have a better capacity to detach and extricate ourselves from the animalistic part of ourselves, i.e. the body and mind. We are not compelled by just our instincts or reactions or a basic sense of survival. If you started to question your life and its meaning, you have touched this level. Remember that these sheaths filter and permeate into one another so you can move from one to the other easily. It is not like a ladder where you move linearly from one rung to the next, in this case, you are moving laterally. Operating at this level means that you are operating from your intuition and wisdom. The measure of how much you operate from this level depends on the frequency and intensity of your spiritual practices. In Western mysticism, this is the level of the Higher Astral Body. Those people who have the skill of astral travelling will use this part of their body to do so.

The final sheath, No. 5, is actually the same level where you are at one with the Soul Light because it is here that you are in the *Anandamaya Kosha* – the *Bliss Sheath*. In Western mysticism, this is the level of the Casual Body. Although the Soul Light is permeating from one individual soul, the Light cannot be held within boundaries so can merge with the Universal or Divine Light (and other Soul Lights). This is the stage where you are literally and symbolically illumined. This is where you connect with The Divine and feel blissful, joyful and peaceful, not in the realm of emotions but in true bliss. When you operate from emotion, there is often a reason for that emotion. For example – you feel happy because you have a good life, therefore the reason for that happiness is that good life. If that good life is taken away, you will become unhappy. But when you are in the state of bliss, there is no intellectual reason for that joy. You could be poor or ill and still be blissful. The state of blissfulness comes from your connection to The Divine. The Light from The Divine is so strong that all your shadows are dissipated. This is the stage of Enlightenment. As I said before, I don't view it as One huge Big Bang of Enlightenment. I feel we are given glimmers of it or rather our increasing spiritual practices will allow us glimmers of this state of insight. Again, don't take my word for it, just practise your various techniques until you can see it yourself. It's the best infallible way. You are not imprisoned by other people's views, you are free to inspect the facts for yourself. This is true liberation.

## Liberation

Liberation does not arrive in a magic potion. It is disciplined work on yourself to rid yourself of attitudes, opinions, false ideas which you have inculcated into your personality. It is separating the Operating Personality (the car) from the Real Self (the driver). When you reach this purified state of knowing, you become aware that your body is your functioning tool through which your Spirit can express itself. Learning about your body and what is contained within it, (not in the biological sense but in the subtle sense) will allow the stuff that is hidden in it, your past traumas, pain and sorrow which are inhibiting your growth to be brought out into the open. This is self-therapy but is not psycho-therapy nor psycho-analysis. You don't need to comb through every minutiae of the past incidents, just the understanding that there were past incidents which may cause you to behave and react in certain ways. Then you engage with The Divine Light to shine on these aspects to allow the shadow to fall away thus freeing you from their dark hold on you. However, if you have a specific incident or issue that is still hooking you to the past, you can work to release that specific pain. (*Mindwork 4* in my book, *Body And Mind Sculpture: Shape up for Self-Discovery* will show you how to deal with this.) In all of this process, you are never alone. You are guided by Divine hands. In Paulo Coelho's story of the Pencil, he stated the first quality of the pencil, "You are capable of great things but you must never forget that there is a hand guiding your steps. We call that hand, God."

Liberation is also not about losing yourself. Some people fear that they might lose the sense of who they are if they start work on spiritual disciplines. In fact, you gain more than you lose. You recover the sum total of yourself. What you achieve through spiritual work is the ability to get into a sacred space. From here, you get the distance you require to look at your Operating Personality Self, the person who has to function in your day-to-day activities. Your ability to distance yourself means that you don't get caught up in the wasteful energy of negative thoughts, feelings and actions that result from  knee-jerk reactions to the things that happens to your Operating Personality. Because you have the knowledge of who you are, you develop a composure or equanimity that you otherwise cannot have. It is this composure that will make you calm and joyful and give you the peace that will otherwise elude you. Nothing can live without Light.

Peace and joy will be yours when you clean up the sheaths that obscure your Light. Letting your Light shine through is the same as healing and  connecting to The Divine Light.

**Something To Do (4):**

Make a list of the things to do which makes you feel truly happy. (It has to be something that does not harm anyone else.). Think of each item on your list and notice how your breath feels, how your body feels, how your mind feels. Engage with the feeling of joy that thinking about those things give you.

Better still, allow yourself to do one of those things.

# CHAPTER 5

# Your Energy Or Vital Force

*"And may you be peaceful and joyful and recognise that your senses*
*are sacred thresholds, May you realise that holiness is mindful gazing,*
*feeling, hearing and touching, May your senses gather you and bring*
*you home"*
John O'Donohue
*A Blessing For The Senses*, Anam Cara

Your Energy system exists in the No.2 sheath, the *Pranamaya Kosha* or Vital Energy sheath. What science calls *energy* is different from what is meant here. In physiology, *energy* is produced during cell metabolism and the burning up of glucose in the body. The Energy that we mean is *Prana* and this is not limited to the body, food nor the material world. This Energy is like the Electricity of your body but is part of the Energy that exists in the Universe and can interact with this Universal Energy that exists in the larger world. Hence in Sanskrit, the latter is called *Maha Prana*, The Great Energy. In Chinese, *prana* is known as *Tai Chi*. Probably Life Force or Vital Force is a better term than Energy to avoid any confusion because this Inner Electricity sustains your life.

Think of your house. All the appliances in the house require electricity to make them work, your computer, TV, kettle, your lights, etc. Think of your body as your house and your organs and limbs as appliances in your house. You need your Inner Electricity, your Vital Force to enable them to work. In the old days, in our houses, we have exposed wires to take the electricity to our appliances. (I am aware that these days there is Blue-Tooth technology which replaces wires and many appliances can function without wires or are wireless but this analogy will not be useful for our purpose so please bear with me.) Once upon a time, these wires were visible in our houses but as we become more modern, these wires were covered up and hidden for aesthetic and safety purposes. So when we flick a switch and the lights on the chandelier hanging from the ceiling come on, it is not readily observable how the switch on the wall is connected to the chandelier at the ceiling. But of course the electrician knows, and we too know that there are hidden wires that carry the electricity from the switch to the chandelier. But a child or say, a new visitor to our planet may not know of the hidden wires and cannot comprehend why flicking on a light switch on the wall can turn on the chandelier on the ceiling.

In the same way, this knowledge of the body's electrical system was perceived by the Gurus. They could *see,* if you like, the *hidden wires* within our pranic body which are obscured from our normal perception. This is our body's unique electrical system. Physiologically, each organ can function healthily because it is fed by arteries and veins which take fresh blood to it and remove the used and tired blood. Arteries and veins, though not visible outside our body, are visible inside the body. However what energises the organs, tissues, musculature and skeleton of our body is *prana* or the Vital Force, which is not visible to ordinary sight. The *prana* runs along the *pranic* electrical wires call *nadis* in Indian and are understood as *Meridians* in Chinese. If you are highly sensitive and you place your hand over a part of an electrical wire running to your computer, kettle or stove, you are likely to feel the heat or pulsing of the electricity running underneath. But if you are not the type to feel this, then it will be that bit harder for you to feel your internal *pranic* centres and wires. But with regular and sustained practice, you can become more sensitive to the subtle energies that exist, you will be able to feel your Inner Electricity. You don't have to worry about people who tell you that *prana* does not exist, you will be able to ascertain it for yourself. You don't have to be psychic to perceive it, simply more in tune with your body, more perceptive to what is going on within yourself. (Incidentally, people who are healers, can feel this in their hands and thus can use it to heal others.)

## The Importance of The Spine

Now we will come to see why the spine in so important in yoga. This is not a physiological lecture but is geared towards helping you to understand the fundamental importance of the spine to help you connect to The Divine though some physiological information is necessary.

Physiologically, the spinal vertebrae protect the spinal cord – an important make-up of your body. Messages from the brain run through the spinal cord through the spinal nerves to every single part of our body. Once any part of these is damaged or in poor condition, the part of the body it feeds is affected too.

In hatha yoga, all of the postures are executed in relation to the spine. Mostly, the spine is encouraged to stretch to give space to the vertebrae and spinal discs. Poor posture due to congenital problems, pregnancy, diseases like polio, the type of work or sport we engage in, or pure laziness puts pressure on the spine by putting it out of alignment. Any misalignment of the spine also affect the front of the body in relation to whether the spine curves inward or outward overmuch from its natural curves. Any deviant in the upper spine affects the chest and its organs, particularly the heart and lungs and functions of breathing; the mid and lower spine affects the abdomen and the organs in the abdomen and all their functions. That is why good posture is so essential to good health, not just good looks.

The vertebrae are separated from one another by spinal discs which act as firm pads of cushions to absorb any shock to the spine. By stretching the spine, space is given for these cushions to be nice and plump so that any shock or trauma to the spine can be absorbed. Poor posture puts a lot of pressure on the vertebrae forcing them to come towards each other and thus the cushion pads tend to splurge sideways causing a condition called *slipped disc*. The degree of this condition can vary and the symptom could be an occasional ache in the back to permanent chronic pain, pain running down your leg as the sciatic nerve gets affected or a full-blown slipped disc condition which requires hospitalisation. That is why hatha yoga postures properly executed are wonderful to ease back pain.

Because yoga postures do affect the outer and inner body and *pranic* sheath, it's essential that you work with a properly trained and qualified yoga teacher or therapist who knows what she is doing rather than a teacher who is only focussed on outward form. The inchoate teacher who learns by looking at the shape the body is making in a posture and then emulating that shape to teach her class is merely touching the tip of the iceberg in yogic physiology. She is not aware of the internal repercussions of those forms or postures. Every posture has its positive and sometimes negative effects on internal organs and the functioning of the body, emotion and mind. A good and experienced teacher promotes the positive effects of the posture and minimise any adverse effects by taking the right precautions and suggesting counter-postures. A teacher who is not properly trained may mouth all the relevant stock-phrases, like chakras and *prana* without the deep understanding that is essential and necessary. She may also be unaware how certain postures, despite all its beneficial effects, can have dire consequences for people with certain physical or medical conditions. Focusing on the outward posture as though it is gymnastic or a kind of aerobic exercise can therefore be dangerous.

The right kind of movement in hatha yoga, together with good breathing techniques, also help to bring oxygen and blood to nourish the spine and to help lubricate the spinal joints. One of the movements we hardly do in our daily life but that's done in a good yoga class with proper observation is the spinal twist which helps the vertebrae and joints to articulate smoothly. (There are many good books on hatha yoga postures so they won't be covered here. My own book, *Body and Mind Sculpture* will show you which postures are relevant for working with the different chakras.)

Yet, despite all these physiological benefits, the yogic postures involving the spine were not designed for its physiological health alone. The postures were designed, mainly to keep the main energy channel open and in good health.

## The Main Channel For the Vital force

Running in the same space as the spinal cord and spine though not visible to scientific exploratory instruments is your main Energy Channel, the *sushumna*. This starts at the base of the spine and moves upward to the crown of the head. Just like the spinal cord, other tributary channels run from this like your spinal nerves to influence every part of the body. Just as the brain sends messages to the whole body through the spinal cord and nerves, The Divine sends Her messages (as such) through the *Sushumna*. The latter is a trunk-line communication cable to The Divine. People often talked about a tingling down their spine, it is the Vital Energy from the Sushumna that is being expressed in your physical body. It is your metaphysical telephone ringing. Next time round when your spine tingles, do answer The Divine call!

Two other major channels are the *Pingala*, Right (Sun/Solar Energy /Ha) the *Ida,* Left ( Moon/Lunar Energy/*Tha*) *nadis* which twist round the *sushumna* at each location of the Energy Centres or chakras (our gateways to The Divine) which we will discuss in more detail in the following chapters. (The symbol of the medical profession, the caduceus is based on this. If you recall, the caduceus has the main staff with two snakes twisting up the staff which has two wings at the top signifying that this was Hermes's staff. The two snakes are actually derived from the yogic idea of the *Kundalini* or Serpent Energy. The serpent is symbolised as lying in our body, in our pelvic cradle shaped like a basin or *kunda* in Sanskrit. Isn't this interesting when yoga was founded in the East thousands of years before medicine became a science? The yogis knew this intuitively but it took science several hundred years to come up with this same symbol.) This Serpent Energy rises when we begin our awakening and is on the spiritual path and we achieve Enlightenment when it reaches the Crown Chakra. These two channels give us the name *Hatha* Yoga as all the posture work will influence the flow of *prana* through these two channels. Any part of your body which is in pain or diseased suggests that the *nadi* running to it is not flowing smoothly or is blocked. A good yoga therapist will assist you in re-establishing the flow of *prana*. A good therapist will be able to identify the areas of blockages and she will suggest postures which will activate  relevant centres to incite a flow of *prana* to the appropriate areas. The yogis of bygone days have designed each posture to put a certain pressure on each of the main Energy centres and nadis using various techniques to stimulate flow to the various channels. This is the main function of posture-work in yoga.

## The Chakras Or Seven Energy Centres

Altogether, there are seven major chakras or Energy centres. These are located along the *sushumna*, your main *pranic Channel*. Although they are located on the spine as such, because each chakra radiates a vortex of energy, they can be felt in the front of the body, which is called their contact points. Interestingly, each of the chakra is located on a physical nerve plexus or an endocrine organ. (Again, you have to bear in mind that the yogis *discovered* these chakras, intuitively, five thousand years before they knew the existence of these organs we call the endocrine organs and nerve plexus.) Therefore the influence of a particular chakra is related to the hormones supplied by the brain or that organ. That is why proper management of these chakras will lead you to improved emotional and physical health. The chakras operate on a finer frequency than that of the physical body. Therefore, when you have fine-tuned your frequency through regular yoga practices, your sensitivity will be enhanced and you will be able to feel their heat and pulsing. There is no magic or hocus-pocus involved, merely a keen awareness of your own body.

The word *chakra* is Sanskrit for a wheel. This suggests the movement of the Energy Centre which is a vortex of energy that pulses and swirls around like the movement of a wheel. To be more accurate, my perception of its flow is that it is more like a *Fireworks Catherine wheel* rather than the movement of a cart wheel, with the Energy scattering in all directions as the wheel turns. The old-fashioned lighted Barber's Pole with its white and red colours inter-twisting with each other is my perception of the Right/Sun/*Ha* and Left/Moon/*Tha nadis*. The Sun represents our masculine aspect whereas the Moon represents our feminine aspect. Each of us has both aspects in our being.

In yoga, the awakening of the three aspects of chakras, *sushumna* and *nadis* are different awakenings with different experiences. Chakra awakenings are pleasant and comfortable whereas *kundalini* or the Serpent Energy awakening through the *nadis* and *sushumna* can be more confusing and sometimes traumatic. Hence such attempts should be carried out with proper guidance from an experienced guru otherwise hallucinations and other problems could ensue. It is **not** the scope of this book to **force** such awakenings.

What we are going to learn about the chakras in this book will help us have an overall understanding as to their location in the body, their basic functions and how they affect us physically, emotionally and psychologically. We will explore broadly some of the associated medical conditions and emotional issues and how we can work with those issues though this book is not meant to be used in place of any medical doctor, professional psycho-therapist, psychologist, psychiatrist or equivalent. (Always be responsible for yourself and consult your medical professional before embarking on any alternative journey if need be.) There are many more details about the chakras that are not mentioned here only because they are not immediately necessary for the purpose of this book. Scholarly students who wish to learn intensively about chakras need to find more scholarly exposition of the subject or from their gurus. The idea in this book is to provide an over-view of the chakras as expressed by different traditions and not just one so that you may have an exposure and understanding of why there may be a different opinion or expression of any of the chakras. The best way for you to know which works best for you is for you to discover the chakras yourself.

That is why the perceptions of these chakras act as only a guide, not a prescription. Allow yourself the freedom of perceiving the *chakras* and *nadis* in your own way. Different colours have been ascribed to each of the chakras as different disciplines has sometimes suggested different colours. For example in a *Kundalini* Yogic perception of the Heart Chakra which sits in the middle of the chest, the chakra's colour is green, whereas it is blue from a Tibetan Yogic perception. (The seed mantra to activate this particular mantra is also different in the two traditions.) To my mind, the colours serve as a visual guide for us to be able to *see* the *chakra* or *nadi* in our mind's eye and thereby giving us a foothold into that inner dimension. If a particular colour has a negative emotive effect on you, then refrain from its use and work with a colour which is pleasing to you. I may be wrong but I feel that the actual colours should not be the cause of dissension in the early stages. After all men are known to be colour blind and the colours attributed to the chakras were first perceived by men!

## Chakras As Gateways Or Portals

As you are aware, a gateway is a portal or an avenue of entry. Besides physical entrances, a portal can also exist in a subtle dimensions and is an opening through which we can access a different dimension to that of our own physicality. (For example Platform 9 3/4 *King's Cross Railway Station* is Harry Potter's portal to the dimension of the magical train station that takes him to *Hogwarts*.) To connect to The Divine, we have to go through the gateways of our physical body. Each of the chakra is linked to a sensory element, emotional and psychological issues. By looking into these issues, we learn to recognise the issues that are holding us back or those who can help us to move forward. The process of identifying these issues and working on the chakras help us to cleanse and purify the chakras, thereby the shadows in these areas can be dispelled. So by focusing on what is taking place in our body, we are gently led into the subtler dimension of the *Pranic* Body or Sheath. Without this transition, our perception will remain *attached* to our physical body and thus we are unable to free ourselves from the erroneous idea that we are only this body. By learning to navigate in the subtler realm, we learn to operate in the finer frequency of The Divine.

The communication is two-way. This means that just as we attempt to communicate with The Divine, The Divine also communicates with us on an individual basis through these portals. (Remember the analogy of the two Tunnel Boring Machines from France and England moving towards each other.) Thus our learning to be aware of our body and our mind is also a means through which we are interpreting the messages sent by The Divine. Of course it is encrypted in the *language* of The Divine. Though I use the term *language* it's not a verbal language just as *body language* is not a verbal language. We know how someone is feeling by the *body language* she is expressing. This type of communication arises from the way the person is holding the body and the way we are interpreting the signs in our heart and mind. So too with Divine language, we have to be in the correct frequency and be able to *interpret* the signals, just as a Morse-Code Reader has to interpret the bleeps he hears. Someone who is not trained to interpret Morse-Code might say that the bleeps do not make any sense. In the same way, a person who has not bothered to learn the *language* of The Divine is in no position to deny the existence of The Divine. Trusting yourself and your ability is a key towards this understanding of The Divine.

## The Gateways and Our Senses

Since there are seven chakras, there are seven portals in our body which are our gateways to the Divine. Starting from the base of the spine (No. 1), we move upwards to the seventh chakra which is located at the crown of our head (No. 7). (We will concentrate on each of these in the following chapters.) Of these seven, five are related to our five senses. On a physiological level, our senses are linked to different parts of our brain which register a particular sensation. Our brain sends a message to the appropriate organ which then responds to the sensation or sense, for example, if it's a desire for food, our brain triggers off a sensation of hunger in our stomach.

But we are not just an animal. That is to say, we are a Conscious being that has the capacity to acknowledge our sensations and withhold our responses. The better we are at not simply reacting to a biological stimulant, we begin to work through our senses so that they do not let us astray. It is possible for us to use our senses in such a way that we go beyond them to apprehend the intrinsic essence of what there is.

That is why in the quote at the top of this chapter, John O'Donohue calls our senses our *sacred thresholds*. In his *Anam Cara*, he was writing about Celtic spirituality. The understanding is no different in Eastern spirituality and particularly in yogic and Buddhistic spirituality. John O'Donohue elaborated by saying that *holiness is mindful gazing, feeling, hearing and touching*. The key word here is *mindful*. To be mindful means that you bring your awareness to what your sense is perceiving at the time. Holiness is not about wearing whatever-coloured robes or cultivating a beatific look. Holiness is about being whole, about being mindful of your actions and what your body and mind is doing. This is pragmatic spirituality. This is the route through which you can be truly holistic or holy, where you can perceive The Divine.

In Chapter 3, we asked "What would be the use of God providing us with senses if we are to deny all of them?" People still have feelings of guilt when they indulge in their senses. We have to enjoy our senses to perceive the beautiful world that The Divine has created. What we need is perspective – perspective to know how not to overindulge our senses to the detriment of our Body, Mind and Spirit. If we are *mindful* whilst we smell the roses and hyacinths; when we taste the clear water of a mountain spring, when we watch the rise and fall of a baby's chest, when we touch the veined hand of an old person, when we hear the sound of the sea, we are using our lower five portals to enter into the space of The Divine.

People who practise regularly do develop a sixth sense and this too will carry us, like a boat into the space of The Divine. This sense pertains to the chakra on the forehead, which is also the location of the Third eye. All these senses are gateways to the Divine but sometimes we are waylaid by the pleasure and thrills that each sense can provide so much so that we forget to use them as portals to The Divine. Each of the following chapters will be dedicated to one portal or chakra so that you can learn more about it and how it relates to your body and yourself. After the seven chakras have been covered, we will look at the *Bija Mantras* or *Seed Mantras* which act like keys to unlock them. Understanding and unlocking the chakras will provide us with the gateway to The Divine.

I won't be telling you what *The Divine* is. This will be prescriptive. There are enough religions telling us who and what The Divine is supposed to be. This is your own special journey of discovery. Though I might use the pronouns *Her, She* for The Divine to avoid a chauvinistic appellation, do use *Him or He* as it suits you. The Divine does not exist in form so is genderless though we can worship Her/His attributes in human form. She does not exist in the gross frequency of physicality but in the finer frequencies. Our verbal language is a type of form thus language creates boundaries and limitations. Therefore to try to define The Divine in any language is to limit it. That is why Lao Tze said in the *Tao Te Ching*, *The Tao that can be spoken is not the true Tao.* Your journey is thus to perceive The Divine yourself so there will be no quarrel and no wars over definitions. True spirituality is not defensive, it does not have to be, it just IS.

---

### Something To Do (5):

Become sensitive to your body's Inner Electricity. You can do this on your own or with a partner. If working with a partner, sit facing each other. Close your eyes. Rub your palms together. Without opening your eyes, turn your palms to face your partner's. Allow the heat and prana from your palms to locate each other's palms. Keep the palms a distance from each other. Don't touch. Just feel the energy between the two of you.

If working on your own, rub your palms, close your eyes and rub your palms together. Then allow your palms to face each other without touching. Feel the Energy between your palms. If you can, feel the direction of flow of the Energy.

---

# CHAPTER 6

# The First Chakra

*"For the one thing I greatly feared is come upon me,"*
Book Of Job, The Bible

Remember that the following seven chakras are the major chakras. There are many other minor chakras, some which we will mention if they are relevant. Not all the minor chakras are named. Remember too that the characteristics and corresponding issues we attribute to these chakras are based on the yogic tradition. It is one interpretation. Of course there are other interpretations and other ways. Work with what is best for you right now.

Just think of where the location of your first chakra is and you can deduce the kind of issues that are connected to this Energy Centre. In the male body, it is in the perineum, between the scrotum and anus; in the female body, it is close to the cervix. Thus this chakra affects the anal muscles, anus and part of the reproductive organs. In Sanskrit, it is called the *muladhara* chakra or Root chakra. *Mula* also suggests a source, a beginning. It is also where our roots, if we were a tree would go deep into the Earth. Therefore this chakra is our first connection between our Energy being to our physical being.

Notice that our English word, the human being is made up of two words, *human* and *being*. Therefore the process of our physical living is to be-ing. *Be* in the present. *Be* in our body. Be-ing.

## The First Chakra And The Physical Body
The health of the basic elements of our body like our skeleton, our bones, teeth and nails are affected by the health of this chakra. It

also affects the pelvic region. So if you suffer from osteoporosis, arthritis and such related diseases, your body is suggesting that you should pay more attention to your first chakra. Since the first chakra has to do with our anchoring to our foundation, deterioration of the skeletal structure which provides foundation for our body suggest that you may have issues in your life where you feel a lack of stability.

By health of the chakra, I mean its balanced functioning. When the chakra is too heated up, you can be over aggressive, defensive, tied too much to material things; when it is too low, you can become too wimpish, ineffectual, playing the victim. But when properly energised, this chakra will make you feel secure, full of energy to tackle life with confidence. So if you want to build up your confidence, work on this chakra. If you want your bones to be strong, make sure this chakra is functioning healthily.

## Our Operating Personality or Ego is Born

The Soul moves from spirit to a physical embodiment through the second and this chakra. The moment we re-surface as a being which possess a physical body, the ego or our Operating Personality is born. This Operating Personality is the identity we use to get on in this world, in this incarnation, for instance, my Operating Personality is *Phine*. (The term here is my own made-up one and so is not crucial but the understanding is. It's the part of us which Operates in order to function with the rest of the world.) That is why, if we are only focussed on this Energy Level, we tend to be involved with having to wrestle with the issue of our identity. Who am I? What am I? What makes up my identity? Therefore this chakra reflects a sense of *I-Am*ness or of our identity in this physical manifestation.

There are many spiritual disciplines which appear to want to get rid of this ego and many New Age teachings advocate destroying this ego. I tend to be more cautious here. If by ego, they mean an aspect of us which is inflated and detrimental to one's spiritual quest, then I agree absolutely. But if by ego, it is meant the personality who has to function or operate in this world then I would contest that this personality is very much required and necessary to operate life on the physical plane. That's why I am calling it the *Operating Personality* for want for a better term to get away from the term Ego which is loaded with so many ideas and impressions.

If there is no strong sense of the Soul existing simultaneously with the Operating Personality (OP), the OP suffers a kind of bereavement, because it has *divorced* itself from its Soul, though it may not consciously know it. The OP feels alone, unsure of who it is. This is the first instance of detachment from our Soul. My understanding is that the more traumatic the actual birth process has been, the more one would have been rudely awakened to one's inception to the body thus severing the sense of attachment to the Soul. This also gives rise to the feeling that nothing exists outside of the Self.

The OP is a gatherer and has to gather from around her to forge this identity which is newly birthed. Besides our DNA and karma which predispose some part of our personality, our identity-kit is slowly assembled by gathering from the circumstances we find ourselves and from other OPs around us, like our mother, father and all who we come in contact with in our childhood and young adulthood and even through our adulthood. So in many respects, this OP is never a complete, fully formed product and has to live through life's rich tapestry of experiences to *be* someone. That is why the OP is always in search of the Holy Grail of the Self, looking everywhere for the sense of Self. But it only has to look within to discover the jewel that it already possesses - the Soul, and become reunited with its own Soul. Unfortunately, the further one travels away from the Soul, metaphorically, the harder it is to get back because one becomes more and more entrenched in the OP and the world it inhabits therefore whatever takes place in it is more obvious. The

Operating Personality and the empirically evident world thus becomes your reality and the less evident world of the Spirit is either overlooked or rejected.

One of the indicators in your body that you've travelled too far away from your Soul is the feeling of tiredness or exhaustion, the sense of lack of time or too much time. If there is no medical reason for you to feel tired, and you are, you have to try to come Home. Home is where your Soul is at. Becoming sensitive to our chakras and being in tune with our body and being Present is a way of coming Home.

Much of our unhappiness is in this frantic search to find out who we are, in the journey to *become* and not stopping to think we are already *be*-ing. When not operating together with the Soul, the alone-ness of the Operating Personality generates a sense of fear, fear of the uncertainty of identity. This fear can be exacerbated by the intrusion of other Operating Personalities who could further nullify what bit of identity you might possess. It is this that we are defending against when we react to others who are trying to destroy our sense of self or who chip relentlessly at this vulnerability. If we are more certain of ourselves and are deeply connected to The Divine, other Operating Personalities have less power to threaten us.

## Chakra Indicator

As the physical body is not separate from the inner sheaths of bodies, our fear is registered in the First Chakra. Think of the operation of a chakra like a thermostat in a room. You turn up the thermostat when you want more heat in the room, you turn it down when you want the room to be cooler. This chakra tends to be red-hot and pulsates intensely when you are fearful. Feel this yourself. This will almost inevitably lead to the clenching of your anal sphincter muscles and will play havoc with your bowel movements. If you try to be too controlled or controlling, you will be constipated. (This is the source of the pejorative reference to people who are called *Anally Repressed*.) If your feel yourself out of control, you will get diarrhoea which is symbolic of the loosening of control. Of course these are extremes but are examples of the likely scenario in a situation of fear.

One way to control your fear is to control it through your mind. But this attempt is intellectual, not emotional. Also, we know that the Mind can be a dictator and is hard to shift, even with positive affirmations, so you have to transcend it through meditation. Merely uttering positive affirmations is an intellectual exercise and its effectiveness will not be Soul-deep. You need to focus on The Divine so that your affirmation is strengthened by Divine Energy. You do this in your tuning-in mode, whether in Zazen i.e. seated meditation or dynamic meditation, either walking or engaged in any other activity like washing dishes. This means that you are *mindfully* repeating your positive affirmations. When you are mindful, you are observing your mind, therefore you are Present. When you are Present, you are not led astray by wayward thoughts.

The other way is to regulate the chakra concerned is through a yoga posture. Yogic posture work that focuses on the lower region of your body and anal muscles puts pressure on the chakra and helps to bring it in line.

## Posture Example

Throughout the chapters on the chakras, we will suggest a posture to regulate the chakra in question. There are many books by eminent yogis, particularly the Sivananda and Bihar School of Yoga traditions, who give excellent examples of postures to regulate the chakras. My own book, *Body And Mind Sculpture* give some suggestions too. The rule of thumb is that the posture should influence or activate the musculature of the body which will then activate the region in the pranic body which is pertinent to the chakra that is being worked on.

An *asana* is a Sanskrit word for a posture. It is different from the Western concept of exercise because it has a transcendental element to it and the attention is not merely focused on the physical body. It is called a Posture and not an exercise because in its execution, there is a sense of *Be-ing*, being in the posture, a state of awareness where you coax the body to adopt a physical form or shape so that you can become aware of its relevant parts. Attention is also paid to the breath to direct it and to see where it flows in the performing of that posture. If pressure is put on a certain part of the body, affecting either the lungs or diaphragm for instance, the breath will behave differently as when it is completely free. This kind of awareness is significant in learning to understand our body and our mood and will be the stepping stone towards understanding The Divine.

By *Posture Example*, I mean that I will suggest one posture. By taking into account the elements of this particular posture, for example, where it is focused on the body and on a particular chakra, you can vary your repertoire by finding other postures which work on the same area in the body thus making your daily practise interesting rather than boring.

To work on the 1st Chakra, start by sitting on the floor. Making sure that there is nothing behind you in case you should fall backwards. Draw your legs up so that you are balancing on your sitting bones. This will have the effect of positioning the chakra towards the floor. The energy body in this position will extend into the ground thus anchoring you. Breathe IN and extend your legs and arms out. Breathe OUT, return to original position. Repeat 6 times. Feel the buttocks pushing towards the floor as if you are trying to push your roots further into the Earth. When you finish, sit with your eyes closed to feel the pulsing of energy in this area.

When you have learnt the seed mantra, you can chant it aloud or silently as you focus on this area. When you have learnt the corresponding colour of the chakra, you can visualise it as you work on the posture. But we will take it step-by-step.

A simple way is to breathe into the chakra and it will naturally adjusts itself, the breath acting like a fire-extinguisher spouting out foam if the blaze is too high, stoking the fire if it is too low. The moment you bring your attention to it, you are already moving into the space of the *Pranamaya* Sheath, (No. 2) and influencing its flow. Trust yourself.

## Positive and Negative Fear

The sensation of fear is not all bad, it's a good tool to make you aware of potential dangers. Only fools don't have any fear at all. It means that there is something malfunctioning in the psychological make-up. But as Susan Jeffries famous book says, *feel the fear and do it anyway.* If you were about to leap off the back of an airborne aeroplane with the fields of England twelve thousand feet below, you would be made of metal if you did not experience at least a nugget of fear in your chest. After all, it is a death-defying feat. Your fear is a cautionary instinct. But as you are a well-trained parachutist or sky-diver with hours of practice, you know that the odds of your surviving is enhanced so your fear becomes a cutting edge of excitement. So it is not the *presence of fear* that is important, it is how you *manage that fear.*

Opposite to positive fear which acts as a warning to save you from some mishap or danger, negative fear paralyses you. Instead of acting as an observer or witness of your fear standing outside of that fear, you have entered into its mouth and go down through its dark belly. You become engulfed, consumed.

The trouble with fear as the quote at the head of this chapter says, "*For the one thing I greatly feared is come upon me,*" is that it can be a self-fulfilling prophecy. The amount of energy you use up to be fearful is as much energy it requires *not* to be fearful. Fear generates a kind of magnetism that will draw to you what you fear just as positiveness will draw to you what is positive. That is why it is essential that you don't build up a magnetic force of fear within yourself. Hiding or running from it only makes it stronger. The way to loosen the hold of any fear on you is to valiantly face it, sword in hand like the one held by the God Manjushri, to slash at the ignorance of that fear. You bring in the Divine Light to shine upon it and thus dispel the shadow of that fear. If it is a fear that has held its hold over you for a very long time, it will take a bit more effort for you to loosen it from you but it will eventually be loosened if you continue to face it.

There is a lovely Indian story about a man who was locked up in a dark cell on a dark night with only a small opening that served as a window. He saw a coiled snake on the floor and he was so terrified that he huddled in a corner, away from the snake, unable to sleep the whole night, keeping his eyes on the snake all the time in case it slithered towards him. In the morning, when the sun rays pierced through the small window dispelling the darkness, he realised that the coiled snake was only a coiled piece of rope. He had been terrified over nothing at all! The lesson shows that if we shine the light, preferably the Divine Light on anything, we can see that we have nothing to fear.

### The Sense Of Smell

By the fact that this chakra is located in the body in the area of our bowel movements, it is not surprising that this chakra is associated with the sense of smell. However smells can both be unpleasant as well as pleasant. In many instances, smells can be indicative of sexual attraction and arousal or of danger, in the animal as well as human kingdoms.

Watch a rabbit when it is experiencing fear. It stops, looks around, its ears are pricked for sound, its nose wriggling in its effort to smell. Hence fear is often linked to the sense of smell, as smell acts as a warning. In the jungle, animals survive better when their sense of smell is strong and they can smell their predators' whereabouts. In our homes, our sense of smell can warn us to the presence of smoke or gas. That is why this chakra is associated with the sense of smell because it is with the help of our ability to smell that helps us to survive.

The OP as a newborn infant seeks comfort through smell. Even before its other faculties are in full operation, it can smell its mother. Watch a newborn the moment its mother carries it. Its head turns around until it snuggles into its mother's chest. It can smell its mother's milk or scent. Even with its eyes closed, a baby can seek out its mother's nipple to feed.

Without our consciously knowing it, we often seek out smells and scents that bring us comfort. Those of us who have lived with someone in close proximity, a partner or spouse will know that there is a special scent that is connected with that person, whether it is the perfume or aftershave they wear, the soap or cream they use, a smell that will evoke that person for us. When someone close to you has departed, it is not just the person you miss but unconsciously, we miss the smell of that person. Of course smells can also be a reminder of difficult times and experiences. Whichever it provokes, the sense of smell does trigger memories and forge them. Understanding where your sense of smell has taken you is a vital aspect of letting go of those memories that bind.

## I Will Survive

Once an identity is birthed, its next priority is to survive. Although it's a popular song based on a physical separation, Gloria Gaynor's *I Will Survive* became such a hit because it rang such a positive note. But survival, focussed only on the emotional and material needs of the body does not engage the Spirit.

If you recall the economist Abraham Maslow's *Hierarchy Of Needs* he said that the basic needs to survive are to have food, to want a home, etc. To achieve this, you have to work hard to forage, fight off predators and maintain your space. Then when you do get the things you wanted, you have to fight to keep them. The not-having (any food, home, etc.) and the having of those things produce a fear that is generated by the thought that you won't be able to get those things or a fear that you will lose them, if you have them. So coupled with the fear of losing one's identity is the fear of our inability to survive.

Both these fears are false fears anyway. One, we already have an Inner identity of the Soul so there is no likelihood of losing our identity; and two, our Soul continues to survive no matter what so there is no real issue of *not* surviving. But the mind engages with our body and with our physical existence and without the illumination of our Soul *believes* that our physicality must survive hence the angst.

Going back to our example of people who go for plastic surgery saying that the latter brings them confidence, they are only self-deluding themselves. No amount of plastic surgery is going to give them the confidence they need because they are so far away from their Soul. If they have surgery done on their face a few years on, they'll have to return to get more done. If they are displeased with their nose, they could be displeased with their ears and so on and so on. All this is an attempt to cover up the emptiness they feel inside. The only thing that will make them truly fulfilled is the connection to their own Soul. Because being in touch with your Soul will give you a sense of fullness which plugs up the hole of emptiness within you.

So to live your life merely to survive is to lead a shallow life. You need to live your life consciously, with awareness, so that you are delving deep into your Soul, connecting to Spirit and The Divine Consciousness. This is where true joy lies. Don't take my word for it, try it for yourself. Once the Soul Light is activated, it is so powerful and illuminating that its beauty will shine through even aged skin, wrinkles, spots, deformities and colour. True beauty is not limited to skin, neither in its texture nor quality. True beauty is luminous and will permeate past the dullness of complexion and eyes. It has such a positive vibe that the Energy of True beauty will touch everyone it comes into contact with.

## Working Through The First Chakra

Working through the first chakra means working through your fear and your sense of identity. When the chakra pulsates, especially strongly, it is trying to make you aware that these are the issues you have to tackle with. Don't be swallowed by the strength of the issues. Don't surrender your power to the fear. Face it. Remain aware. Observe what form the fear takes. Observe what is happening in your body. Witness. Be present. Be. The moment you do this, you are taking charge. You are not allowing the old emotions to be like wild horses that take you away from your Presence. Smell something pleasing, something that gives you joy and makes you calm. You are pulling back any power you have surrendered. This is self-empowering.

## The Associated Element – Earth

Generally, each chakra is associated with an element and in this case, the element is Earth. This is so appropriate since our Energy body extends beyond our physical body and can permeate the Earth. Therefore, problems in this chakra will make you disconnected with the Earth, with nature. The red of the earth will link up with the red in your base chakra to ground you. You will be a like a tree with its roots spreading into the earth, anchoring you, making you feel safe, will give you the zest for life. You will feel firm in the foundation of your True Self. Use your sense of smell to ground you to the rich loamy smell of Earth and then to take you through the gateway or portal to connect you to the Divine.

## The Associated Colour - Red

This chakra is often seen to be red in colour, a vibrant red which is also the colour of the Earth Energy, the first colour of the rainbow. (Don't imagine a dull red but one that is fresh and bright.) Red is an alive colour, nourishing. Blood, which keeps you alive and healthy, is red. But an over-stimulated chakra of red can become adverse, think of *seeing red*, the *red flag,* making the bull react with anger. So the balance and tone has to be correct.

Breathe IN through your chakra and imagine yourself breathing through the colour red. Use the imagery to allow you to connect back to the earth. Breathe OUT, imagine your breath going into the Earth. Better still, walk amongst trees, feel the Earth beneath you. Watch the glow of a sunset to connect with that energy of red.

## A Cautionary Note Here.

Many people who are in the pursuit of Enlightenment tend to focus on the upper charkas and not the lower charkas as the upper chakras function in the spiritual dimensions. But if you are not grounded properly and are not capable of handling psychic experiences like being clairvoyant or astral travelling, you could end up being psychotic. All lower chakras must be purified before the rise of the *kundalini* (or serpent energy) to the higher chakras. The Serpent Energy has to rise from the *kunda* or basin which our pelvic girdle represents. The first chakra it has to pass through is the *Muladhara*. Bypassing any of the grounding chakras can lead to emotional and mental instability. For your own sake, no short-cuts, please.

**Something To Do (6):**

Treat yourself to something red. In the East, red is a lucky colour and wards you against evil. A Chinese bride wears red for her wedding. If you have a fear within yourself, wear a red top, scarf, top, skirt or dress. If that fear is connected to your home, buy a red candle to light in your house, a red lampshade that shines red around the room. Grace your home with red flowers, a red ornament or picture. Red keeps you grounded and safe.

Have something that smells nice in your house, a natural smell if possible, like a fragrant hyacinth plant, roses or tiger lilies, incense.

## CHAPTER 7

# The Second Chakra

*"A poet, an artist, a painter is on the way to becoming a mystic.*
*All artistic activity is on the way toward becoming religious."*
OSHO
*Creativity, Unleashing The Forces Within*

Our Operating Personality is created and birthed from this chakra. The location of this Second Chakra is thus in our reproductive and urinary organs. In particular, this chakra is connected with sex, creation, creativity and excretion. The chakra is located at the base of the spine at the level of the coccyx or tailbone and thus is sometimes called the Sacral Chakra. Its contact point on the front of the body is approximately three fingers width distance below your navel. (This is not prescriptive, it is only a guide. Discover yours for yourself.) In Sanskrit, the chakra is called the Svadhisthana Chakra, *Sva* meaning self. It is in fairly close proximity with the First Chakra thus the two chakras have inter-connective issues. So this chakra, too, like the first chakra has to do with our sense of who we are and what we are. As this is the location where we are created in the womb, it also has to do with our relationship with our mothers and for women, our relationships with our children. As it is a sexual centre, it also has to do with our sexual partners. Tibetan Yoga has a discreet way of addressing this chakra, calling it the *Secret Chakra*.

### The Second Chakra And The Body

In the body, the Sacral Chakra affects the reproductive organs as well as the urinary organs like the bladder and kidneys. As the latter has to do with the excretory process of the body, the energy of this chakra also affects blood circulation and the lymphatic system through which the body dispels its toxins and waste.

Every time cell metabolism takes place and when you exercise, lactic acid is being formed. If we are breathing in the yogic way whilst performing an exercise, the breath on exhalation removes the lactic acid to flush it into the lymphatic glands. That is why good breathing techniques are so important during exercise. If you don't breathe out well during exercise, lactic acid that forms will remain in the muscles and could develop into cramps the next day.

## The Creative Force

The creative force of this chakra touches not just the reproductive and physical levels but also our mental and emotional levels. So besides creating babies, this chakra is responsible for the creative arts, for your desire to paint, draw, play music, write, etc. These reflect the positive side of this chakra which makes you feel alive and enable you to produce wonderful music and other works of art. However, at this chakra level, the art or music we produce can still be at a more craft or pedestrian level. Only when our creativity is linked to the intuition and creativity of the 6th Chakra does the work become that of a real artist and genius. The first three chakras which are in the physical dimension are co-related to the last three chakras in the metaphysical dimension.

When this chakra is activated, there is a huge surge of energy to accomplish things. A person's enthusiasm and joie-de-vivre comes from this centre. A lack of energy flowing through this chakra can result in inertia and being listless and bored.

The sexual nature of this chakra means that sexual power is vested here. When the energy here is flowing smoothly, one's capacity for sex is wholesome and is an experience that can lead you closer to another human being and ultimately to the Divine. In Tantric Yoga, the sex act, between a man and woman is used to heighten awareness thus taking the couple to direct experience of The Divine. This process, called *maithuna,* is not an excuse for free indiscriminate sex but is a process which involves specific cleansing and devotional rituals to prepare the body and mind in a disciplined way to use the sexual union to burst through this gateway, moving from physicality to spirit.

In a true, loving sexual union, both persons are Present in the Now. If a partner is engaging in fantasy whilst performing the act of sexual intercourse, she is not Present in the Now but is somewhere else. This is a betrayal of your sexual partner and objectifies him, using his body for pleasure but without real emotional or spiritual connection. When this chakra is not purified, sex is used as a means to some end or as power itself, controlling others through the giving of sex (or not) and being aggressive in sex. A volatile out-of-control chakra could result in the person using sex indiscriminately with all and sundry to prove her sexuality. In actual fact, it is proving her insecurity and it is also a form of self-abuse. Connected to the issue of identity as per the First Chakra, at this level, the sense of identity will revolve around oneself as a sex object. Thus women who have the need to make themselves out as more sexy by having their breasts enhanced have unresolved issues about their self-image. If they have been pressurised by their partners to do so, then their partners too have problems with *their* self-image.

Sex, the idea of sex and sexual relationships can generate feelings of jealousy, feelings of guilt, feelings of lack of control, of being used, etc. That is why it is so important to get this chakra to be in balance and harmony. In understanding this chakra and its operation, we learn how to respond when it engenders feeling of lust. Instead of responding like an animal, we pause, take stock and allow the sexual energy to take us into a finer dimension. This is a process of transmutation where your mind is removed from the thought of mere copulation. Yet when you do have a partner who respects you, this energy can be used for expressing love at a deeper level and for taking you closer to The Divine.

## Chakra Indicator

If the fear of the First Chakra is not resolved, it is exacerbated through the second Chakra as well. So one becomes motivated by fear. Therefore the act of procreation, of having children, is done not because one loves children but one is afraid of being alone or feels annihilated as a species if one did not have them. Sexual intercourse on this basis is also done because one is afraid of being alone, of not having emotional and physical contact. Of course, all these are germinated at an unconscious level and may not be perceived by the Conscious Mind.

In addition to fear, this chakra has, obviously to do with desire. This desire is the desire to have, to own – either people or things. If the *kundalini* energy is focussed on this centre and does not move on, then the person can become very lustful, material-istic and/or possessive, amassing material possessions and people they can control and manipulate. So greed is a great indicator that this chakra is not refined.

That is why the Yogis say that this is the hardest chakra for the *kundalini* energy to pass. In both yoga and Buddhism, desire is seen as the main culprit that causes our unhappiness. When we desire something or someone, we are not happy until that desire is fulfilled. Even when that desire is fulfilled and we get our car, money, mansion or partner, the unhappiness is only dissipated for a while and then will return because we discover that the achieving of that particular desire did not make us happy after all. And so a new desire is born. Sadly, even in the talent of creativity, desire can be a pitfall as we want to do better and better at our art propelled by our insecurity and what others might think of it. That is why depression plagues many creative people and the former is another symptom that this chakra is not in good functioning order.

Of course there is negative as well as positive desire. Negative desire promotes the ego whilst positive desire promotes the happiness of others, like the desire to help people in need, and the desire to make the world a better place.

The Yogis also tell us that all our past acts, traumas and experiences are remembered and stored in this particular chakra. These tend to block the energy and won't allow it to pass through the gateway so that we are unable to access the Divine. Therefore, for us to be able to move on, this chakra needs to be cleared.

## Posture Example

A very good asana to regulate this chakra is the pelvic tilt because the muscles can be engaged through contraction and release to stimulate the chakra. Acupuncture stimulates the flow of energy in the meridian through the manipulation of a needle. Yoga does the same thing. The meridian is the medium which carries the energy, much like a wire carries electricity. A *meridien* is a Chinese concept and *nadi* is an Indian concept and it carries the body's electricity. The two lower chakras are the two easiest to be stimulated by muscle control.

Though this posture can be done in a standing posture, I would suggest, for safety reasons, since you are unsupervised, to do this from a lying down posture. Lie down on your back with your legs bent, your feet resting on the mat or floor, arms by your side. Take note of your lower spine resting on the mat. The region we are working on is between your tailbone and the navel. Breathe IN, push your tailbone into the mat by arching your lower back. Your lower back should lift from the mat. Breathe OUT, push the lower back into the mat, pull your tummy muscles in very strongly, including your anal sphincter muscles (and if you are a woman, your vaginal muscles as well). Relax. This is one round, repeat for 3 rounds and rest. (**Caution**! Do not practise this asana when you are pregnant, when you have your period or if you have any disease in this region.)

Besides working on the 2$^{nd}$ chakra, strengthening the muscles of your nether regions will help prevent or reduce the problem of incontinence. This will also alleviate lower back pain problems if the pain is due to bad posture.

## The Sense Of Taste

Our comprehension of many things in this world is through our sense of taste. A baby finds comfort through tasting the world through its mouth, first by grasping the mother's nipple and later by putting objects into its mouth. The symbol of our love and affection for another human being is a kiss. Though a platonic kiss includes the sense of touch, it has an element of taste when one kisses a cheek. Certainly the sense of taste becomes much more evident in a sexual kiss which involves lips, tongue and saliva contact. In a deep French-type kiss, the couple almost seem to be eating and tasting each other.

Taste is a powerful sense that allows us to perceive texture and flavours. Obviously taste is associated with food, a substance which we need to survive. Thus the issue of survival is still very close in this $2^{nd}$ chakra. More often than not, the taste of food is associated with its smell, the first sense from the first chakra. Food is such a fundamental part of the human make-up that the taste of our childhood food will stay with us a long time, whether for positive or negative effect. The memory of that sense could connect us to the happy times in our childhood or the difficult times. Adults in the UK who were post-war babies, for instance, have an aversion to tapioca because it was served in place of potatoes just after the Second World War. And they loved chocolate because they were deprived of it. Often, no matter how adventurous one is in relation to types of food, one tends to return to the foods of one's culture or nation when in a state of emotional stress or need. That is how the term *comfort eating* came about. It is eating to satisfy an inner emotional need. People who become overweight through eating can lose weight not by tackling just the weight aspect but by tackling the emotional issues which cause them to over-eat through working on this particular chakra.

But taste is not just limited to food but to our abstract sense of taste that pertains to our taste in types of people, fashion, the arts, sports, entertainment, religion – in effect the whole gamut of social activities and emotions. It is our taste that differentiates one Operating Personality from another, much more so than physical differences. It is the variety of tastes which gives life its excitement and colour. However extreme differences in taste can also breed distrust, dissension and wars. So use your sense of taste to revel in the wonders of nature and allow that sensation to lead you back home to The Divine.

## I Will Enjoy

If basic survival needs like having a home and food have been taken care of as indicated by the 1st chakra, the strongest emotions that are prevalent at this level pertains to the idea of enjoyment or its lack. Because this chakra has to do with desire and taste, it's about appetites of all sorts, food, sex, excitement, thrills, drugs, etc. It is the *I Will Enjoy* maxim. Its opposite is, of course, the *I Cannot Enjoy* or *I Will Not Enjoy*, i.e. people who have difficulty in enjoying themselves or people who feel that enjoying themselves is a sin. Some people use their *not enjoying themselves* to punish others, their spouse, their children, etc. It can be a powerful manipulative tool. Others cannot enjoy themselves because they have such a burden of responsibility which they inflict upon themselves.

One client I worked with in yoga therapy believed that the purpose of his existence was to ensure that his family was comfortable and happy. He did this by supplying them with money and material things and in the process forgot that they had lessons to learn in life for themselves, or that money alone could not make people happy. He felt alive only when there were problems to tackle and when he was needed by others. He aborted therapy work because if therapy was successful, he would be free to do his own thing and to enjoy life, rather than working for others and, sadly, he could not cope with this notion of freedom and joy. And, yet, his body knew that he was not happy by having severe backache and pains in the chest and shoulders.

The energy of this chakra could swing from enjoyment to the other in the same person whenever guilt comes in to remind the person that he is not supposed to be happy.

The combination of the sense of taste and desire can be quite volatile and can lead to excessive enjoyment of foods, thrills, excitement, drugs, etc. thus leading to addictions and additive inclinations. If this happens it suggests the disturbance of the energy in this chakra and measures have to be taken to calm it down.

Denial of the propensity and energy of this chakra is not an answer. Denial will lead to subversive desires. So if you deny your sexual needs, the suppression could be damaging and could come out in aggression and other negative expressions. That is why in Tantric Yoga, the opposite is recommended, that you satisfy your senses fully. In this case, it will mean active fulfilment of desire and taste. The idea is that you can have only that much sex or that much food after which you will be sated and would then move on. In True Tantric Yoga, engaging fully in desire and taste is coupled with other inherent disciplines of yoga practices which will reduce the harmful effects of the indulgence in desire and taste, practices like watchful breathing, mindful observation of the self. Too many people seize the aspect of indulgence in Tantric Yoga and do not use it to forward their spiritual journey. The gateway to The Divine is thus blocked because the aspirant is caught at its gross level.

## Working Through The Chakra

When the chakra is fired up, it pulsates as well as produces heat. This heat and pulsation is felt in the body, in the sacral region if you are really sensitive. But even if you are not, the fact that the chakra is located around the vaginal muscles, the clitoris or the penis and scrotum is that the sensation in these parts activates the brain to think about sex and food, not necessarily in that order of course nor at the same time. We often act on the desire to have food. (Interestingly the desire from food does not originate in the stomach but originates here.) The fulfilment of that desire for food could be necessary and not harmless though taken to excess, it could be harmless. However the desire for sex, if one is without a spouse or partner could lead to all sorts of complication and angst. Often the desire for sex at this level is lust and is not love.

The important thing to realise is that one does not have to react to the chakra stimulation. If you merely act every time this chakra is stimulated, you are reacting on the level of the animal. This is why being Present and in the Now is such an important concept worth attaining. When you are Present, you have the capacity to stand back from the stimulation that is going on in your nether regions, be mindful and notice it but also knowing that this is taking place in your physical body but not in your True Self. The moment you are able to do this, you create the distance necessary for you to use this chakra as a gateway to The Divine. In this manner, when you do react to the stimulation of this chakra, whether it is in the realm of desire or taste, you can enter into the energy of the chakra and enjoy something wholeheartedly and sincerely. The joy comes from recognising that The Divine is in all things and brings about all things. So when you are absorbed in what is created by The Divine, you too are taken to heights of creativity. When you are captured by creativity in this chakra, you are open to inspiration and to The Divine whisperings. It is in the moment of Creative Inspiration that you are closest to The Divine. Brilliant artistic people, like great composers, artists and writers can exhibit this ecstatic moment in their works. When people listen to their music, see their paintings, read or hear their words, they will be moved into exquisite joy thus experiencing what the artist had experienced by entering the same portal that was open to them. That is why Osho and many other teachers have said that creativity is a gateway to mysticism. The chakra's energy act as a booster rocket to propel you through the gateway to The Divine. The trick is to remain fully conscious in the experience and to move beyond an emotional response into a mystical one.

## The Associated Element – Water

The element associated with this chakra is Water. This is obvious as the urinary system affected by this chakra is about water and its excretion. Drinking lots of water will be effective in keeping your system properly flushed and your urine light.

On a psychological level, try to live your life in the flow – like water. This means that as an OP, you can live your life with Presence but without getting caught up in emotional situations. Remember too that gentle flowing water is as influential as rough, tumbling water. The energy of flowing water can shape the banks of a river and can divert its course.

Water reminds us too that we must not mistake form for its essence. Water in different states of solidity takes on different forms. It can be manifested as actual water itself, ice, clouds or steam. The form changes but the essence remains that of the essence of water. In the same way, the Divine might be seen in different forms, God, Jehovah, Allah, Krishna, Kwan-yin, a bird, a tree, the clouds, the rainbow, etc but the essence remains the same.

## The Associated Colour - Orange

The colour normally associated with this chakra is Orange, the 2nd colour of the rainbow. Orange takes on the mix of the colour Red from the first chakra and the colour Yellow from the next chakra, the Solar Plexus chakra, so it means that the issues of all three chakras are interlinked in various ways. Orange is a vibrant colour and in the Chinese culture, Orange is associated with Luck and Good Fortune. Probably why Chinese Buddhist monks wear yellow-ochre robes reminiscent of Orange. Although the Solar Plexus chakra is normally associated with the sun, the 2nd chakra too has a colour that is often seen in the rising sun although it is also reflected in the setting sun. So it is a chakra that can be earthy and joyous. It connects us to the earth through the Red of the 1st chakra, through the roots that take us into the foundation of our planet and of ourselves. This will then make us feel anchored and safe to explore the further reaches of our inner landscape and help us on our journey towards The Divine. When you are in need of solace, you need to connect to The Divine. One way of doing this is to watch and experience an occurrence in nature, like watching the sun rise.

---

**Something To Do (7):**

Be bold to express your creative urges. If you want to play music, play. If you want to paint, paint, if you want to sing, sing. Don't let others or the fear of how it might turn out deter you. It does not matter how well or not well you do it, just do it. By doing what your inner you is telling you, you are accessing your inner rhythm. Through expressing your inner rhythm, you will express your inner beauty and the song of the universe which will take you closer to The Divine.

# CHAPTER 8

# The Third Chakra

*"To see your drama clearly is to be liberated from it."*
Ken Keyes, Jr.
*Handbook to Higher Consciousness,*

This chakra is our power centre, the engine room of our physical and pranic body. It is here that our food is digested to become fuel for our body. In yoga, this is seen as the Fire Centre because we require the fire to metaphorically *burn* up the food for it to be come fuel and energy. So this chakra is responsible for generating energy throughout the physical as well as pranic bodies. This chakra is located in the region of our Solar Plexus and digestive organs. In Sanskrit, the chakra is called the *Manipura* Chakra, which is a combination of two words, *mani* meaning *jewel, pura,* meaning *City,* literally the *City Of Jewels.* So this chakra holds a wealth of treasures. In the Tibetan tradition, this chakra is called *Mani Padma; padma,* meaning *lotus,* therefore, the chakra is also considered as our *Jewelled Lotus.*

## The Third Chakra And The Physical Body
As each of our bodies is different in body-length, I feel that the best way to locate this chakra in your own body is to place your palm flat against your body, little finger at the navel. Just above where your thumb is should be the location of the *manipura.* Another way to gauge its location is by closing your eyes to sense its pulsating. This is one of the strongest pulsating chakra as its work of digesting the food requires a huge amount of energy. Think of the sounds and heat of an engine room, say on board a ship or power plant and you can visualise what is taking place in

your body manifested by this chakra.

In certain traditions, this chakra has been called the *Navel Chakra*. I personally do not perceive it to be right at the navel so this is something you have to ascertain for yourself. I am aware of the energies of the Second and Third Chakra interacting at the point of the navel but perceive my Third Chakra to be a little higher up in the body. But this is not prescriptive since chakra detection is not an empirical science but an esoteric science which is hinged on our perception and intuitive sense.

As the chakra's energetic influence is in the solar plexus, you can visualise it as your inner sun. Its active functioning will provide you with inner sunshine and warmth. Without the sun, trees and plants will not grow. Much of the Earth's creatures will be adversely affected if the sun does not shine. In countries where there is a severe shortage of sunlight, people suffer from depression and melancholia. In the same way, it is important to ensure that your inner sun is healthy and strong.

The condition of this chakra affects the stomach, the liver, the gall bladder, the spleen, pancreas and intestines. Though the kidneys are in this region too, they are more associated with the 2nd chakra which has to do with the urinary system. Besides digestion, the organs in this area have to do with the purification of the body, i.e. cleansing the blood and getting rid of toxins. The liver's job is to break down the physical and chemical toxins in the body. On an emotional level, our emotional toxins of anger and jealousy are stored in the liver. Many words in our English language to describe our emotions come from the organs of this region e.g. *You have the gall to...*; referring to the gall bladder; *She tasted bile*, bile being the bitter secretion of the liver and stored in the gall bladder, released into the duodenum during digestion to emulsify and absorb fats. In archaic terminology, bile is one of two bodily humours, *Black Bile* which was thought to produce *Melancholy* and *Yellow Bile* which was thought to produce *Anger*. Another example of English usage: *I have butterflies in my tummy*, to indicate nervousness or anxiety. Therefore mood and emotions are expressed in this centre and not at the heart centre, as is often believed.

## Expression Of The Operating Personality

This chakra actively expresses our Operating Personality and has to do with how we function in relation to others. How we express ourselves is dependent on whether we have tackled the issues surrounding the lower two chakras, i.e issues of our identity and our sense of survival. If neither of these has been resolved, we will use the energy of this chakra to wield power unnecessarily or we give away our power and become victims to others. This power struggle takes place here. Notice what is happening in the pit of your belly when you meet certain people.

You may have had occasions when you meet someone at a party or social gathering and afterwards feel empowered or drained. This is because the person you came into contact with has the capacity to impart or draw energy from you through this chakra. A positive person will impart their energy to you whilst a negative, needy person will suck it out of you. The latter is sometimes seen as a *psychic vampire*. In the latter circumstance, you will do well to protect yourself by closing down this chakra before you go out and enter a crowded place.

## Chakra Indicator

As this chakra has to do with power, excessive energy here could result in several problems. If the issue of the sense of identity has not been resolved, this, combined with the force of the energy here will diminish the sense of Self. The latter could lead one to a sense of insecurity or an inferiority complex which makes one act in an arrogant and controlling way. A monumental ego is one of the effects of an over-strong solar plexus chakra that is not in balance. The arrogant ego stands in the way of our relationship with The Divine as it will not recognise or acknowledge a power beyond itself.

More often than not, habits are actions we automatically engaged in without thought as we have been doing them for years. Habits are like muddy tracks we travel on. The more we travel along them, the deeper the groove we cut into the tracks. To use a modern example, our repetitive thoughts and habits are lasered onto the tracks of a CD so that we tend to replay the same tune again and again. This repetitive action accentuates our OP and the habits become the identification marks of your OP. The more these habits are enforced, the further you will be taken away from your Divinity. So in order to find your True Self, you have to switch from being an automaton instigated by habits into a being who is mindful and aware. If you want to change your life for the better, you have to change your CD tracks.

This chakra, rather than the heart chakra, is considered to be the emotional centre as the heart chakra's emotions are of a higher nature. Emotional insecurity and problems are manifested as diseases in this region. The most common one is a high acid content in the stomach. Acid is produced when there is anxiety. The *butterflies in the tummy* syndrome is an initial indicator and when not controlled, lead to severe anxiety that results in gastritis and eventually to a gastric ulcer. When someone is highly stressed the adrenals pour out adrenaline which tends to draw blood away from the digestive system, weakening it and making it prone to diseases. Other forms of ulceration in other areas of the digestive tract suggesting this similar emotion of anger are manifested as colitis, IBS (Irritable Bowel Syndrome), Chrons Disease, hernia, celiac, etc. If you have any of these, your body is suggesting to you that you need to tackle deeply imbedded emotional issues so that you can release them before this chakra can be a gateway for you to comprehend the Divine. Food, alcohol and drugs addictions are also generated from this centre. More often than not, the addictions are an emotional response to fear, insecurity or unhappiness. That is why eating disorders like bulimia, anorexia and obesity stem from the malfunctioning of this chakra and correcting its balance will help in alleviating the illnesses.

Although the body's rate of metabolic activity is conditioned by the thyroids in the throat, it begins here where the energy is first generated. Therefore the amount of energy you do or don't possess is dependent on how efficient your digestive tract and organs are working and on a pranic level, how your prana is being generated and distributed. People who suffer from low energy levels with illnesses like fibromyalgia, MS etc tend to suffer also from low self-esteem and thus have to look at the issues that caused them to cede control to others.

There are more specific types of prana that operate in the body. The five different pranas operate in specific places in our body but it is not essential to know the various names and details unless you are studying the *Science of Prana* called *Prana Vidya*. It is sufficient to know that the chakra here is the source of your body's vital energy.

It is important to balance the energy here if you want to pursue your Life's Purpose. There is a wonderful, positive energy emanating from here if the balance is right. People who have strong but balanced *manipura* energy give out very positive vibes and are charismatic. If you have tackled many of your old emotional issues, the free flowing prana will result in joy and spontaneity.

## Posture Example

This is the third and last chakra that can be properly stimulated through a physical posture or muscular contraction. This posture is quite strong. So, if you suffer from any digestive tract problems like ulceration etc, this asana is best done under supervision. If you are undertaking it yourself, be responsible and sensible. Use it with care. This is **not to be done** if you are pregnant, menstruating, have any internal bleeding, a full stomach or any serious abdominal problems. Find a gentler alternative or, better still, find a good teacher or therapist.

Sit on the floor with your legs stretched out. Make fists of your hands and put them on your body just above the navel, knuckles pointing upwards. Breathe IN where you are. Breathe OUT and bend forward as far as you can go, allowing your fists to push into the belly to stimulate your *Manipura Chakra*. Breathe IN, return to Starting Position. Breathe OUT. Relax with eyes closed. If you can manage it, do two more rounds. Then sit quietly and take your attention to your Solar Plexus chakra.

## The Sense Of Sight

Very interestingly, the *Manipura Chakra*, rather than the chakra located near your physical eyes, is associated with the sense of sight. Sight is a very powerful sense which we use to act upon the desires of the lower two chakras. In fact sight often leads to desire being generated. If you see a good-looking woman or man whom you desire, the desire began with your sighting. If you recall, *desire* is an aspect of the 2nd chakra. You see food and the desire for it then develops. If sight is not properly controlled in this aspect, it is like a runaway horse that takes you hither and thither, where you race around merely fulfilling the desires that your sight has engendered. Yet, sight can be useful as it warns you of dangers, the survival issue of the 1st chakra. It is these connections that make the *maniupura* chakra still part of the earthly chakras.

Sight is linked to emotions as the sight of a loved one can move you to joy or someone you hate can move you to anger. The sight of someone or something can evoke all other sorts of emotions like understanding, prejudices, fear or loathing. It is often through sight that our judgements arise. Our view of others take us back to the issues of the lower two chakras if our judgement is based on our fear and insecurity or our experience of that person. For example, a person of fair skin might judge a person of dark skin incorrectly based on the fear of the 1st chakra because his sense of survival is threatened.

On another level, sight is seen as *insight*, the ability to *see* beyond the ordinary. Although insight begins here and is rudimentary, it becomes far more developed in the 6th chakra or the Third Eye Chakra which is located between your two eyebrows, near your physical eyes. At the *manipura* level, insight as such is instinctive, a more animal level. This gives rise to the saying, *gut instincts* as the sense is located in the belly. Although it is important to heed the warnings of our instinct, we also have to learn to unlearn some of them if the instincts lead us to emotional imbalance. Some of our gut reaction can be wrong because the gut reaction is a result of a pattern of behaviour that came from our childhood. For instance, if we have been abused by an adult as a child, the child in us will react instinctively in an adverse manner if an adult shows signs of strength. What is essential here is to bring in the wisdom of the 6th chakra so that instinct becomes insight.

This is the level at which we can use our inner sight to observe ourselves, i.e. observing what is going on within our body and our mind. By being witness to yourself, you learn to separate what is your vehicle and what is really You. You will start to loosen the identification you have with your Body. You are no longer shackled to it nor think that your Body is you. Understanding this, you will be able to manage The Body better, knowing that it is your tool for spiritual progress and not allow its desires and needs overwhelm you. You gain a wonderful perspective and freedom from its ties.

Linked to the creativity of the 2nd chakra, sight can allow us to appreciate beautiful paintings, art, music, landscape and encourage us in our creative endeavours which are the strengths of the second chakra. The purification of the Solar Plexus chakra allows us to see wisely and to use what we see for the benefit of all mankind.

## I Will Be Strong

In the same way that you learn to develop your physical muscles for physical strength, you need to develop your emotional muscles to be emotionally strong. You can do this by regulating your *Manipura Chakra* so that the fire within is under control. A strong emotion like anger suggests too much fire in this area which means it can burn you. Anger is also very corrosive. That is why when someone holds a lot of resentment and anger, it results in diseases that corrode the physical body, ulcers, cancer, etc. People can also be resentful if they believe they do not have power. In this case their fire is too low so there isn't enough energy to assert themselves and they become victims or suppress their own needs. Suppressed emotions are unhealthy for the *sharira*, i.e. the body+mind+spirit. They take up space in your psyche, blocking the nourishing flow of Vital Energy. The anger must be released so that it does not become toxic. Being present when you experience the anger, together with the practice of hatha yoga is a very good and effective way of releasing the anger, thereby the toxins that poison your body, mind and spirit.

As the *Manipura Chakra* deals with power, emotional and moral strength is generated here. What is important is that strength, whether it is physical or emotional should not be used against any other person or against oneself. Strength can be soft and gentle, the type that overcome difficulties but is not damaging. For example, nuclear power is very strong and is very useful, provided it is used in the right way. Power wrongly used corrupts and becomes a dictatorship. Strength that is hard is directed against oneself or others. When used properly, the fire and strength provided by this chakra makes the person an achiever. If the upper chakra of the heart is in good functioning order, it can provide all the right motives to achieve. This sort of person will then be an asset to herself and society, using her talents and qualities to fulfil her Life's Purpose.

In the introduction, we said that when you are expressing your special gifts, you are not being selfish; you are expressing The Divine because doing so will bring you closest to the Divine. If you are expressing your gifts in creative ways like in music, art or writing, you too can help bring other people to the threshold of The Divine through your works by inspiring them as we had mentioned earlier. You will help others to glimpse the portal that you have walked through. In fulfilling yourself, you are able to assist others to open their own gateways to The Divine.

## Working Through The Chakra

The combination of power and sight is very potent. Used correctly, the energy of this chakra can help you to work through your emotional issues to bring you to harmony and self-control. Swami Sivananda in his book, *Health and Hatha Yoga* said that many *people are slaves of impulses hence they do not enjoy peace of mind.* By bringing your emotional responses into balance and control, you will be less of a victim to impulse. Although spontaneity is a result of the activation of this chakra, it does not necessarily lead you astray into impulsiveness. Spontaneity is an active, positive response whereas impulsiveness is an auto-knee-jerk reaction that is not always positive.

In the quotation at the top of this chapter, Ken Keyes, Jr. said *"To see your drama clearly is to be liberated from it."* This means that if we can be Present to whatever is taking place in our mind and emotions (as well as our physical body), we can liberate ourselves from the emotions that tie us to our Past History. We don't have to buy into the drama of our Past. Remember the Third Quality of Paulo Coelho's pencil, the pencil allows an eraser to rub out what mistakes had written. So if we can use our sense of sight to metaphorically look into ourselves, our minds and our hearts, we have a greater chance of emancipation. Liberation is not a Never Neverland concept, it is for here and now. Painful experiences which culminated in painful emotions are hooks that snag at our emotional flesh drawing blood. We need to be able to unhook each one slowly. Of course pulling out a hook will mean a small amount of blood is spilled in the process, meaning that there will be some emotional blood-letting, but ultimately the place where the hook had been will heal. It cannot heal if the hook is never pulled out. Being in a place of strength means that you have the power to take out the hook and liberate yourself.

As we mentioned above, the energies of the second Chakra and third Chakra is felt at the navel centre as well. As this was the location of our umbilical cord, working on this chakra does bring up issues relating to our birth-mother who nourished us in our foetal state through this conduit. Whether or not you have been brought up by your biological mother, her contribution to your birth has to be acknowledged and resolved, otherwise you will develop a kind of neediness which will make you possessive in your relationship with others. Mother-daughter issues too can be worked out if the two chakras concerned are balanced.

Issues with others, particularly painful or hurtful ones means that one has not let go of the person involved, whether one is still with them or not, whether they are dead or alive. This is an attachment. You are not free. If you are not free, it means part of your heart is in shadow. To allow The Divine into your life, you need to be able to love wholly. That is why working on this chakra, in cleansing and purifying it will help you to use it as a gateway to The Divine.

## The Associated Element – Fire

If you bide by the old adage that *Fire is a good servant but a bad master*, you will ensure that you can use the energy of fire in a useful way but will also know how to control its blaze. One of the ways of regulating the fire is through your diet. Both the Indians and Chinese believe in the yin-yang of foods, certain foods that stoke up the fire and certain foods that do the opposite. For instance spices stoke up the fire and cucumber cools it down. Aryuveda is the Indian system of diet and medicine which help to regulate the prana in the body. There are many good books on this subject if you need greater details.

Instead of focusing only on the food we eat, it is far more important that we are able to absorb the right food. There is not much point in spending a huge amount of money to buy the most expensive food and vitamins if the body is unable to absorb it or simply discard it as waste. For instance, one of the main reasons why smoking tobacco is bad for our body is that the presence of nicotine affects the absorption of Vitamin C. So you may eat all the best fruits and take the best quality Vitamin C but if the body cannot absorb it, it will be a vacuous exercise. The right balance of pranic fire will help in the processes of digestion and absorption.

There is tremendous will-power associated with this chakra, and like fire, will-power can be hugely useful but too much can result in the person being wilful, arrogant and over-competitive. However, people who develop this chakra properly can be great leaders in their field. They are the kind of people who follow a path of self-development and realise their full potentials because they have fire in their belly. Such people tend to be very charismatic and their energy is infectious and can serve mankind.

## The Associated Colour – Yellow

The colour associated with this chakra is the third colour of the rainbow – yellow. Think of a bright and fresh yellow like lemon or the noon-day sun. When the sun gets up high in the sky, it loses the orange-redness of the rising and setting sun, which are the colours of the lower chakras. Each colour of the rainbow suggests the colour that precedes it or follows it. Therefore since each chakra is not an island unto itself and is a moving vortex of energy, the colours are merged at some level.

When you feel low or listless, get out into nature and connect with the living things around you and the pure air. Breathe in the oxygen and the joy. Feast your eyes on yellow flowers, daffodils, buttercups, roses, sunflowers, etc. Look at a chirpy yellow canary or bask in the glow of a golden yellow full moon.

---

**Something To Do (8):**

Live your dream. What have you always dreamed of doing? Did you want to try to sky-dive, climb a mountain, ski or swim with the dolphins? Find the adventure of your dreams which will make you immeasurably happy. Then do it. Don't let fear stop you. If it is money that stops you, set something aside each week. Or do an extra job so that you can achieve your dream. Someone once said,

*Don't let your dreams die*
*When dreams die,*
*It's like a winged bird that cannot fly.*

Let living your dream take you nearer to The Divine.

---

# CHAPTER 9

# The Fourth Chakra

*"One can overcome the forces of negative emotions, like anger and*
*hatred, by cultivating their counter-forces, like love and compassion."*
His Holiness, The Dalai Lama
*The Art Of Living*

This chakra is at the boundary between our Earth and our
Spiritual chakras. Although the physical heart sits slightly to the
left of our body in our chest or thoracic cavity, the Heart Chakra
is right in the middle of the chest. Its Sanskrit name is the *Anahata*
*Chakra*. The word *anahata* is often interpreted as *unstruck* or
*unbeaten*. In Sanskrit esoteric knowledge, the Heart Chakra
expresses the unstruck sound of the Universe, a sound that is
unbroken and always flowing. This aspect is manifested in the
biological heart which beats continuously from birth and is
broken only at death.

## The Fourth Chakra And The Physical Body
Since the biological heart deals with the circulation of blood, our
Heart Chakra is responsible for the circulation of Energy or prana
around the body. After the work of the digestive tract is done,
where food has been digested and absorbed and becomes fuel for
the body, it is taken into the physical heart which acts like a distribution factory, sending the nutrients in our blood to where it is
needed in the various parts of the body and brain. The latter
involves the energy of the Solar Plexus or Manipura Chakra
leading into the energies of the Heart Chakra. Oxygen supply to
all our organs and tissues and the removal of carbon dioxide are
other functions of the biological heart. So the maintenance of the

vitality of this chakra enriches the flow of blood and prana around our physical and pranic bodies.

The Heart Chakra sits directly in the region of the thymus, an endocrine gland, which produces lymphocytes and antibodies which are the components of the body's immune system. When we are children, the thymus gland is as large as a fist. But this gland tends to atrophy, hence the reason why our immune system declines with age. Therefore the proper functioning of this chakra has tremendous influence on our immunity level as well as our lymphatic system, the system that gets rid of stuff the body does not need.

Closely linked with the movement of our Energy is our breath. Therefore the Heart Chakra is also involved with the organs of breathing, the lungs, trachea, bronchus, intercostals muscles, diaphragm and the whole respiratory system. Breath is the medium which takes you through the gateways of the chakras to The Divine. That is why all movements in Eastern exercises like yoga and Tai Chi are done in cooperation with the breath. Your breath as prana takes you from the physical realm into the metaphysical realm. Attention to your breath is not just a focus for its own sake but is a way of moving beyond the thoughts generated by your mind so that you can step beyond it, out of its way to perceive The Divine.

The breath allows your pranic body to expand just as it expands the intercostal muscles and lungs. When the body is under stress, the breath is contracted and so too is the pranic body. To awaken to spiritual consciousness, we need to loosen up our breathing, to make it more generous and expansive.

## Seat Of Love And Compassion

This chakra is the seat of love and compassion. The love that is expressed from this chakra is of a fine and spiritual nature. It is not love that is motivated by sexual impulses, fear nor insecurity. Therefore the emotions that emanate from this Energy Centre are much finer than the lower emotions generated by the lower chakras and particularly by the Solar Plexus or Manipura Chakra. Where love emanates from the lower chakras tend to be possessive, the kind of love here is unconditional and encompasses all beings and humanity and is not restricted to oneself and one's family. The Buddha, Jesus Christ and all the other Enlightened Masters exhibited this great love. The Chinese philosopher, Mo Tze, called it *Universal Love*. He was less popular than Confucius who lived in the same period because he was misunderstood. Confucius advocated filial love and Mo Tze upset people by saying that it is far more important to practise *Universal Love* for everyone than to practise only filial love to one's family.

This higher kind of love gives birth to compassion, a caring for others. You can be compassionate about other people's suffering without getting caught in their drama. To be compassionate is very healing. Your consideration for others before yourself is returned a hundredfold in graces to you. As the Dalai Lama said in the above quotation, love and compassion can help us to overcome negative emotions, particularly those of hate and anger. The words Dalai Lama in Tibetan means *Ocean of Compassion*. He is considered a Boddhisattva, an Enlightened Being, who has reincarnated to help others get on the Path. He emphasised that compassion is the key towards understanding ourselves and others. Hate and anger are very corrosive and are more damaging to the one who feel it than the people to which we direct that hate and anger. This does not mean we cannot feel anger at injustices done. In the first place, we have to be honest with ourselves and asked if what we called injustice is justifiable. Even if it is not, any injustice done to us becomes an opportunity for us to practise compassion. We deal with them by looking at ourselves, acknowledge this anger and release it from us in a positive action rather than holding on to it

## Chakra Indicator

The obvious physical indicator of this chakra is the way the person opens or doesn't open herself to others. On a physical level, when shoulders are rounded and closed as if they were trying to protect the chest area, there is an indication that the person is trying to protect herself as if the chest holds a soft centre. In the upper physical body, this creates a curvature to the upper back as in kyphosis in which the neck would jut forward like a turkey's neck, the head over the line of the shoulders. Internally, this suggests a compression of the lungs and the diaphragm which would then affect breathing capacity and quality. More than not, a person exhibiting such physical traits tends to have problems with their breathing, have asthma, emphysema etc.

Emotionally, a person holding such a stance tend to cower in life too. Either they fall prey to the power of others because they lack confidence or they use their emotions as a controlling bargaining tool as in the conditional giving of love expecting mega returns.

Diseases which affect a person whose Heart Chakra is not functioning properly tend to be diseases that affect the immune system, like allergies, infections and auto-immune diseases like arthritis etc which suggests a imbalanced functioning of the thymus. AIDS is also a disease that suggests the lack of love that results from a blocked Heart Chakra. Being overtly possessive, critical, both to oneself and others, is a clear sign that this Heart Chakra needs work. The shadow emotion of this chakra, is attachment. So someone whose Heart Chakra is not open properly is attached to people or material things. To be too attached to other people means that one's happiness and survival are dependent on them. Your world is built around others and you cannot exist as a whole person without them.

When this chakra is actively open and working in good balance, the person will be very loving and compassionate and will give love unconditionally, i.e. loving without expecting returns. Such a person tends to smile a lot and have a cheerful disposition and will spread joy to all she meets.

## Posture Example

Tightness in our chest muscles and the shortage of our breath are general indications of the contraction of the Heart Chakra. As the shoulders and neck are inter-related to the chest, tight muscles in this area will also affect the chest and upper back. People who suffer from asthma tend also to have tight muscles in their chest, making their breathing laboured. An asana that expands and stretches the muscles in the chest and shoulders will be of great help to them and to those who need to re-energise their Heart Chakra. Gentle stretching with focused breathing will slowly expand the thoracic cage and give room to the organs in the chest. It is far better to do repetitions of expand-and- rest, expand-and-rest rather than enforced over-stretching in one session that might force the muscles to retaliate by refusing to budge. If the emotional heart has been contracted a long time, gentle coaxing is much more effective. To open the Heart Chakra entails a kind of vulnerability hence it's tied in with courage to do so.

You can sit, kneel or stand for executing this posture depending on your ability to stand firmly on the floor. Fold your arms into your chest, palms facing your chest, fingers pointing towards each other, elbows at shoulder level height. Imagine that your folded arms are the folded wings of an eagle. Breathe IN, open your wings as if you are about to take flight and allow your arms to stretch until they are straight and your palms are facing forward. Maintain the arms at shoulder level. Breathe OUT, return to starting position. Repeat three more times.

When you understand the posture better and are more confident, you can add more expansion of the chest and back muscles by tilting the head slightly back to look upwards when your arms are fully extended. But BE CAREFUL. Do this only if you are stable on your feet, or knees. Also DO NOT do this without supervision if you suffer from vertigo, high or low blood pressure, neck problems or glaucoma.

Any other posture that will expand the chest can also be used.

## The Sense Of Touch

There is such magic in the wonder of touch. So much love can be conveyed through this sensation, whether it is that of a mother to her child or that between people in love or just friends and even between strangers. Often it is this lack of touching that makes a person lonely. The act of hugging and embracing is a socially acceptable way of touching between good friends and family. A simple embrace can be so emotionally nourishing. Sadly, this is what is missed when a person is alone or has to live alone. Sometimes the people who go in search of sexual companions or engage in indiscriminate sexual conquests are in truth looking to be nourished through the sense of touch. Some people fulfil their need to touch by having pets. For lonely people, the pranic energy of their living pets can be of huge benefits to their psyche.

It is no wonder that this sense is connected to the Heart Chakra which is responsible for love at an unselfish and deep level. Obviously when we think of touch, we think of hands which do the touching. The Buddhist bodhisattva, Avalokiteshvara represents compassion and wisdom so she is represented with a thousand arms with a thousand hands, with an eye on each palm (the latter signifies her wisdom. She is actually non-gendered and has been referred to as a *He* in different traditions). The Hindu Lord Shiva and the Goddess Lakshmi too are depicted with multi-arms and multi-hands which exhibit their love and compassion.

Touch has a very healing quality, at emotional, psychic and spiritual levels. This is because, hands, like feet have minor chakras in their middle. (Hence reflexology is so effective because it stimulates the feet chakras.) The Gospel talked about the time when Jesus washed the feet of the disciples. He was not just making sure that their feet were cleaned, he was cleansing and stimulating their feet chakras to open them in preparation for when he sent them Divine Energy which he expressed as *The Holy Spirit*. Hindus genuflect and kiss the feet of their Gurus and Masters to receive the divine Energy coming out of their feet chakras. When I was at Osho's ashram in Nepal, I saw people genuflecting and touching the spot where Osho's feet had rested. It is believed that his Energy prevails even if he had physically past over. Many Christians touch the feet of the statues of saints, perhaps not everyone understood why. Both Hindus and Muslims genuflect and touch the feet of their elders as a sign of respect. It is these chakras that connect us to the Energy coming up from the Earth. That is why many Asians do not wear shoes in the house so that they can draw up the Earth's energy from the ground. (Besides other feng shui reasons). It is a good practise to activate your feet chakras by learning to walk barefoot, particularly out in nature, like on the sandy beaches or on grass.

The hand chakras move in swirls around your palms and are used for healing. That is why healers use their hands to heal (though they don't always have to touch physically), the healing or pranic energy radiating from the centre of their palms. This idea is also expressed in the Christian tradition. If you look at pictures of Jesus Christ, the Madonna and saints, you will often see them extending their palms towards you, rays of light emanating from their hands. Often you can estimate the Pranic Energy of a person when you shake their hands. Although hand-shaking developed as a custom to indicate that there is no hidden knife or sword being held, the quality or lack of in a handshake reveals a lot about the character of the person as well.

People who don't like touching or to be touched are often afraid to lose themselves to the intimacy of touch, for fear of being rejected. This tends to suggest the contraction in this person emotional heart centre. Sometimes such people have been betrayed by the sense of touch, by those who use it in unacceptable way or abusively towards them, i.e. the sensation of touch infused with desire coming from the lower chakras. Sadly, it will take a long journey before such people can learn to trust others to touch them.

Yet, we can use the wonder of touch to help us feel the essence of things. Instead of just keeping touch at a sensory level, we can connect touch with our mind to bring the mind to a standstill. Look at young toddlers touching objects and feeling their shapes. You can touch a flower to feel the tenderness of its soft petal, or feel the texture of a sheep's fleece or a baby's skin or your lover's skin to take you into a deeper experience. When you go beyond the physicality of what you touch, you are touching the essence of The Divine.

## I Am Open

People who have a need to close their emotional heart centres are afraid of being rejected and hurt. This could stem from their being rejected and hurt in the past. So they wear a shield or carapace As this chakra is the boundary between the physical world and the metaphysical, the closure of this chakra can act as a fortress to block your spiritual efforts so that you are unable to move forward. In the language of *Kundalini Yoga*, the Kundalini Energy is stuck here therefore spiritual progress cannot be made. It is imperative for this gateway to open so that the energy can pass through to the higher chakras.

Obviously a fortress protects. But a fortress also keeps out. What is open tends to be vulnerable hence many people choose to shut their hearts so that they do not become vulnerable. But learning to trust the Universe, to trust other people, we will be assured that being open will not invite pain only but also huge joy and love which will not come if we are not open. It does not mean that when our hearts are open, we do not experience pain but we will learn to develop an emotional balance and learn how to steer through emotional storms by getting out of them. If you are caught in a heavy downpour, you have a few choices. You can get wet. Or you can open an umbrella over your head or better still, you can get out of the rain. Only a fool will stay standing in the rain and complain about getting wet, (unless you enjoy getting wet at appropriate times.) The balance achieved when you open this Heart Chakra will give you the capacity to weather any storm. You learn to be compassionate but not attached to the emotional situation. This is not coldness or indifference but is equanimity. It is this equanimity that will allow you to be still in any raging emotional storm and through the stillness, you will find The Divine.

## Working Through The Chakra

A contracted emotional heart is an indicator that this chakra is not in balance. Too often, we are still carrying emotional baggage from the past. This in turn makes us create a carapace of protection to stop our soft centre being hurt. Unfortunately this protective shield, if worn for a long time, also rebuts love and compassion that others want to bestow on us. This means we don't allow others to love us as they would like to; and because they can't love us, we then feel that we are unloved or unlovable, confirming to ourselves that we cannot be loved. The 16th Century Spanish religious writer, Juan Pablo Valdes said that the *greatest obstacle to love is the secret fear of not being worthy to be loved.*

This is such a painful and vicious cycle. The cycle can only be broken if you take the risk of letting go of old emotional suffering and allow the healing to occur which emanates from other people's love and compassion. You need to trust the Universe for healing to take place. The carapace cannot be lifted off in one swoop because the hardening has occurred over years, each time you experience hurt and suffering you cement one more layer over your heart. Therefore the healing too will be in several stages; first a crack occurs, then the broken carapace breaks off in bits the more that you trust. And eventually your emotional heart is healthy and whole again, is open and will expand.

Through this expansion, you are letting in the Divine Light. Up until now, your emotional heart has been in shadow, parts of it atrophying from the lack of Divine sunlight. The Divine Light is sustenance for our subtler bodies, just as sunlight is necessary for all physical living things. Think of the effect of the lack of sunlight to human beings which result in different emotional disorders, like melancholia and depression, and you will realise that the lack of Divine Sunlight will result in psychic disorders or malfunctioning.

This chakra teaches us that if we cannot love ourselves, it will be impossible to love others. Hence the idea of compassion is not just for others. It is therefore imperative that we have to learn to be compassionate towards ourselves in the first place and love ourselves, not in a narcissistic manner but in a spiritual mode. You cannot give away money that you don't have. In the same way, you cannot love others when there is no love in your heart for yourself. Only when we can love ourselves and others can we hope to create real changes in the world through change in ourselves first.

Like all the other chakras, one of the ways of working on the chakra is by meditating on it using its Seed Or *Bija* Mantra which will be mentioned in Chapter 13.

## The Associated Element – Air

It is not surprising that this Heart Chakra is associated with the Element of Air. After all, our respiratory system which is controlled by this chakra is about air, its quality, its inspiration and expiration. Like water, air has movement and fluidity. But unlike water, air is freer to move than water. Air does not only have to move within the confines of river banks or bronchioles and lungs. In most of Eastern medicine and systems of healing, air can move freely about the body as well. In Sanskrit, this form of air is called a *vayu*. In both Indian and Chinese healing methods, the way we control our *internal air* or *wind* is through proper nutrition and exercise. If air is static within the body, it creates feelings of bloatedness and is injurious to the health of tissues and organs. As air is related to prana or chi, the positive flow of air within the body will energise and revitalise the whole body and the various other bodies or sheaths, thus influencing our emotional and psychological bodies.

Obviously we need to breathe in air from the atmosphere. The quality of this air is also responsible for the degree of our health. If the air we breathe in is polluted, then our lungs will be polluted too. People who smoke or live with smokers, and those who live in highly industrialised regions, cramped cities with traffic fumes and those in hazardous professions exposed to polluted air, suffer more ill-health than those who live in regions where the air is clean and pure. That is why taking time off to go to the sea or to the park and countryside is necessary for good health. And of course exercises like a brisk walk through clean air will also invigorate and energise the body's system as well as the pranic system.

It is not an accident that the intake of air is called *inspiration*. We can only be inspired when we are in a relaxed and creative state. We cannot be relaxed and creative when our body and mind are in tension, our muscles tight, our breathing constrained. It is when we are breathing in generous intakes of air that our facial muscles relax and the tension dissipate from our muscles and in consequence our physical and emotional bodies. This is our natural Botox! We don't need rat poison to take away the wrinkles from our foreheads – just good, energised breathing!! Prana works miracles to muscles so if you want an effective face-lift without surgery, make sure you breathe well! Later on, we will talk about the effects of chanting as well. That is why smokers tend to have a deathly hue to their facial complexions, their clogged lungs mean that there is very little intake of air and thus energising prana so they look sallow, making them look years older than their actual age.

When we are inspired by the beauty of a sunset, the clouds in the sky, a beautiful landscape or a work of art, we are closest to The Divine. In that moment, we are standing at the threshold, the gateway, the portal. If we relax into that moment and allow it, we will know The Divine.

## The Associated Colour – Green

The colour associated with this chakra is the 4th colour of the rainbow – green. Recall the time you look skywards up at a tree on a sunlit day. See the sunlight streaming through the green leaves giving them the lightness and freshness of life. That is the green you want to relate to when you think of this Heart Chakra, not a green that is dark and heavy but one which suggests new life and vitality.

If you've had experienced any blockage in this chakra, think of fresh air sweeping through the stagnant cobwebs of your emotions and allow regeneration to take place within you. Visualise a new green shoot sprouting in your Heart Chakra as you let in the light and the air. Walk amongst verdant fields and trees. Tap into the energised power of nature. Spring into new life. Walk amongst the hills, spread open your arms and sing *the hills are alive with the sound of music* or its equivalent. Feel the wind in your hair, the grass against your legs, the smell of wild flowers in your nostrils. Let your heart open to the wonder of nature and of The Divine!

---

### Something To Do (9):

Hug somebody. Do this with unconditional love. Don't expect any returns. Just give of yourself. Allow yourself to open. Step into someone else's space and allow them to step into yours. Trust. Be grateful. Be.

If you can't find someone, hug a tree. Feel its energy and vibrancy.

---

# CHAPTER 10

# The Fifth Chakra

*"In the higher realms, every sound, thought, and spoken word
produces strong effects, so it is important to learn to communicate in
loving ways"*
ORIN, as channelled by Sanaya Roman
*Spiritual Growth, Being Your Higher Self*

The fifth chakra is at the base of our throat. In Sanskrit, this
chakra is called the *Vishuddha Chakra*, from the word, *Vishuddhi*,
which means *pure*. Therefore what emanates from here is
generated with purity. This is the first of the three chakras that are
often considered to be the Upper Chakras which suggest that its
functioning is related more to the metaphysical realms than the
other chakras.

## The Fifth Chakra And The Physical Body
The chakra sits in the area of our cervical plexus. This is also
where our thyroid and para-thyroids are located. The thyroid
gland controls our body's metabolism. It is not only the amount
of food you eat which determines your weight but your metabolism rate. If your metabolic rate is low, what you take in is not
used up efficiently for fuel so the tendency to put on weight is
greater and you are apt to feel tired more often. Whereas if you
have a high metabolic rate, the food you eat is digested quickly
and used up as fuel so you tend not to put on weight and seem to
have a huge amount of energy. Of course the balance must be
right otherwise one can be too thin if the metabolic rate is too
high. This could also make the same person very hyper and
unable to be still whereas the other who has too low a metabolism

will have little energy and be too indolent, unable to exert herself to do anything.

This chakra also affects the tongue and vocal chords, the throat, oesophagus (gullet), larynx, trachea (windpipe) and areas of the mouth. (Teeth tend to be more affected by the First Chakra which has to do with our bones and skeletal structure.) As this chakra is located at the base of the neck, it also affects the carotid arteries which send fresh blood to the brain. Contraction in the neck and shoulder muscles affects this chakra and the health of our brain and therefore our whole body.

Bearing in mind that each chakra is not completely isolated in that its spiralling energy is not contained within a box, the energy of this chakra also affects the chest area and its various organs, i.e. the heart as well as respiratory organs, and to some extent the diaphragm. Due to this chakra's close proximity to the Heart Chakra, some traditions say that the Throat Chakra is actually responsible for the lungs and bronchioles. Indeed the trachea passing through to the bronchus, the main channel of the respiratory system, is all connected so it is hard to say where one ends and the other begins. However for the purpose of focus, we would go with the tradition which suggests that this chakra is more closely associated with the throat area.

### Seat Of Language and Communication

The level of consciousness of this chakra pertains to language and the way we communicate using language. This communication is not restricted between ourselves and the outside world but also our internal communication with ourselves and what we tell ourselves about ourselves. Hence the learning from this chakra will reveal ourselves to ourselves which is an important step towards liberating ourselves from the untruths we tell ourselves, and/or others. Therefore Truth is an important factor pertaining to this chakra.

If we are clouded by the Ego, our expressions tend to be

guided by the expression of our Ego-Identity or our Operating Personality. Coming from this limited view-point, we interpret people and situations from this narrow perspective and thereby tend to make erroneous evaluations and judgments. The latter is an untruth which we tell ourselves about others. Either our judgment is based on actual past events with that person or is based on experience which has distorted our lens through which we look. This is internal mental communication that has gone awry. Unfortunately what we then express verbally becomes influenced by what we have judged of the person and situation. Although there are good and happy memories, most of our past situations keep us in pain and hurt. Therefore understanding our past with renewed clarity will free us from this pain and hurt.

As this chakra is concerned with purity, the Truth of what we speak is therefore important. The energy of our words are propelled by the strength of this chakra so it's imperative that we watch how we speak and the manner in which we propel our words into the ether. As Orin said in the quote at the top of the chapter, every word that we utter has a very strong effect. This is also the message of other Enlightened Masters. Although we may believe that what we said has been said and gone, the spiritual understanding is that the *energy* of what we said does not disappear but remain in a kind of *etheric storehouse*, like a kind of spiritual cloud. So it is up to us to contribute to the negative or positive cloud that hangs over all of humanity. As you are aware, clouds are formed by gathering droplets of water. So too our spiritual cloud draws in *droplets* of the energy of thoughts and words.

Think about something that affects us globally and you get an idea of what is meant by the etheric storehouse. For instance the September 11 event generated fear, insecurity and even hatred. Due to a strong visual image of the event broadcast all over the world, the incident affected our Heart Chakra and our Solar Plexus chakra (the latter has to do with our sense of sight). Since that incident, our etheric storehouse is filled with fear and many other negative emotions. Notice how the death of Princess Diana caused an emotional upset that is far beyond what would be considered normal reactions of strangers. This is because people tune in to the energy of sadness and pain that is in the etheric storehouse and connecting with it create a greater force that link them to other people sharing the same emotions. Using the same analogy of a cloud, watch how a small cloud draws in other clouds to form bigger clouds. This is what is also happening at an etheric level. So what may seem to be an isolated feeling, emotion or thought is actually not isolated as it gathers up energy with other feelings, emotions and thoughts in the ether producing larger clouds of similar energy-force. Understanding this principle, we have to do our best to minimise the damage we do in posting negative energy into the etheric storehouse and do our utmost best to influence positive change by putting out positive energy.

## Chakra Indicator

The general indicator of this chakra is in the person's energy output, whether the person gets tired easily or not. Of course a person's physical energy level is not just due to metabolism but other factors like the health of her liver, heart and other organs are to be taken into account as well. But if the thyroids are not in working order, then it's a signal that the pranic flow through this chakra is malfunctioning.

Problems with the throat, vocal chords and voice box are indicative of stuff that has not been expressed. Sore-throats might suggest that communication with one other person or persons is not getting through and the person trying to communicate thus suffers a sore-throat. Perhaps a different way or manner of communicating is being called for. Those who cough are trying to clear some kind of blockage. This person could be subjected to years of suppression where she was unable to express herself.

Coughing is an attempt to get rid of that suppression.

The timbre of the voice often gives away the internal state of the person. This is because this chakra is linked to the 3$^{rd}$ Chakra, the Solar Plexus Chakra. In one yogic tradition, a circle is drawn linking two corresponding chakras which have interconnective energy and issues. The 1$^{st}$ Chakra is linked to the 7$^{th}$ Chakra, the 2$^{nd}$ to the 6$^{th}$, the 3$^{rd}$ to the 5$^{th}$. The Heart Chakra sits in the middle of these concentric circles. Using this idea therefore, the emotions of the 3$^{rd}$ Chakra are expressed through the energy and voice of the 5$^{th}$ chakra. If the expression cannot occur, then the 5$^{th}$ Chakra remains blocked. This is manifested sometimes as speech impediments like stuttering and stammering.

## Posture Example

Yoga asanas which exerts a compression on this chakra stimulates and activate this chakra bringing the flow of prana into balance. Some of the postures which are very effective, like the *plough* and *shoulder-stand* are not easy for most people to perform properly. But if you are familiar with them and do not suffer from neck problems or blood pressure problems and are confident, you can give them a try.

For many people, a simple neck-stretching and rotation will suffice. For safety purposes, begin this movement from the lying down supine position where your head is resting on the floor so that no strain is exerted o the neck. This is important because the neck carries our head which is the size and weight of a heavy ten-pin bowling ball. Lie on your back, shoulders relaxed. Make sure the back of your neck is stretched, your chin is close to the chest. (If this causes a strain in your neck or shoulder muscles, put a folded blanket under your head. A folded blanket is better than a foam block as it has more give and will not be so restrictive. A raised chin is always an indication that the neck muscles are strained.)

Breathe IN where you are, as you breathe OUT, turn your head to your right. Breathe IN, return to central position. Breathe OUT, turn your head to the left. Breathe IN, then back to centre. Repeat 5 more times. From the centre position, breathe IN where you are, as you breathe OUT, lift your head slightly and push the chin towards your chest. Breathe IN, return your head to the floor. This can be challenging, so repeat 3 more times only.

If working from the floor is easy for you and you know that your neck is not weak and you do not have any problems in the cervical spine, you can perform the above asana in a sitting or standing position. In this instance, your head is not supported so do it with care and do it slowly.

In general, it would be correct to say that we are unable to control our throat chakra muscularly. However I have worked with Tibetan yogis who managed to withdraw their throat muscles to produce the sonorous chanting that they are so well known for. This is quite a difficult technique to master as it involves holding the chin down whilst pulling at the muscles at the back of your throat. In combination with the mantra OM, this is a fantastic way of stimulating the throat chakra. However we will discuss the effects of mantras on chakras in a chapter of their own.

## The Sense Of Hearing

This chakra is the last of the chakras which express themselves through our bodily senses. As this chakra is where the voice-box, the instrument of sound is located, it is not surprising that this chakra is related to our hearing as well for without sound, there would be nothing to hear. So therefore you could say that our ears, the instruments of hearing, would also be affected by the energy of this chakra as well although the ears tend to be more associated with the 6th Chakra.

In communication between two people, what we hear is not always what is being said. We often extrapolate on the words that are being spoken. We infuse the words with our emotions and our past history which the speaker may be unconscious of and may not have intended.

Sometimes the choice of words obfuscates meaning. That is why Lao Tze said that *"The Tao that can be spoken of is not the real Tao."* This means that The Divine cannot be easily captured by words.When this chakra is in good functioning order, one can fine-tune the way one expresses oneself and the way one hears. So the faculty of hearing is not just about listening to speech or sound but to the finer meaning of the speech and sound. This faculty is not limited to the words and sounds we hear outside ourselves. Since thoughts are expressed in words, hearing what we tell ourselves and what we think of others is an important tool for uncovering our true self. If we continually think we are worthless, the verbal message we are sending ourselves is that we are worthless. This is what we continually hear. Through recognising the impact of our words on ourselves and on others, we can re-programme our thoughts and re-shape our words about ourselves and others for better, positive purpose. Modern Neuro-linguistic Programming developed from traditional spiritual practices which focus on the way words, whether voiced or unvoiced can influence our physical body, through our muscles, nerves and cells as well as our emotional body.

Hearing is also essential for us to appreciate good music and poetry. People who are musically and poetically inclined have also developed not just their outer hearing but their *inner hearing* so that they can detect the lyrical sound and rhythm of words and music even before they are manifested in our physical world. Beethoven, for example who was born deaf was deaf in his external ears but not his internal ears because he still can hear music that comes from within or that which is expressed in the celestial. Otherwise the music he composed could not have emerged. Enlightened Masters too have this capacity to tune into the celestial music when they are deep in meditation. It is the inner hearing which takes you into the metaphysical realms and thus is important to cultivate.

Of course this chakra also reminds us that sometimes we do not wish to hear the truth, perhaps of ourselves or of our situation. So we develop a kind of selective deafness whereby we only hear what is palatable to us.

## I Can Speak My Truth

Speaking one's truth is the essence of this chakra. This means that you are coming from your real and authentic self. Unfortunately in our journey through life, more than not, our authentic self has been waylaid. Instead, we pick up garbage that is not ours and make it into our own: attitude, traits, mannerisms, needs, wants, even goals. We are so inundated with what others want for us, what they think of us that we begin to believe that this is what we want too and worse, what we are. Generally, we are shaped by our insecurities and fears. So the energy of this chakra invites us to take time to return to the innocence of our being before we had been manipulated by others' and our own thoughts of our identity to re-discover our true self. We can only know The Divine when we know ourselves first. That is why the path towards The Divine is a path of rejuvenation of our own authentic self. Then the truth we speak is our own truth which actually comes from The Divine. That is why this chakra is an important gateway to The Divine.

So people who suppress the truth of themselves are suppressing the truth of The Divine. That is why it is imperative for us to work on ourselves if we want to be on the spiritual path. Without working on ourselves towards positive change and discovering our true essence, whatever we utter from our own false self is only a falsehood. We may wear the external cloak of spirituality, i.e. having the appropriate accoutrement like a beatific look, robes, prayer beads, etc. but if we have not found our authentic self, we cannot be true nor can speak our truth. To this end, it also means that we have to guard against suppressing those who need to express their truth, even if it is going to be uncomfortable for us.

## Working Through The Chakra

If we have developed a kind of selective deafness whereby we only hear what is palatable to us, working on this chakra will free us from our limited hearing and allow us to hear the truth. We have to examine our feelings to see what is holding us back and use our intuition to break out of the prison which has walled us in. Therefore working on this chakra will stimulate the Heart Chakra which is concerned with feelings and the 6th Chakra which is concerned with intuition.

The process of learning our own truth and the truth of the Divine is a long process, sometimes of self-study, intuition and guidance from others, teachers and Masters. We cannot hear or take on the advice of any of them if we do not continuously try to be open to hear them. The Bible spoke of seeds falling on stony ground which meant that the seeds would not have the facility to germinate and grow. The seeds are the spiritual advice that is given by our teachers and gurus. If we do not hear, then it is as if their words (the seeds) are falling on stony ground. You can be seen to attend all sorts of spiritual events and retreats but if you don't open your inner ears, you are not listening properly and thus not absorbing what is necessary for you to hear. Working on this chakra is like removing the stones from the soil and ploughing the earth to prepare it and make it ready to receive the seeds, to create the right conditions for us to hear the words that are spoken by the Masters to guide us to The Divine.

For there to be something to hear, there is sound. For there to be sound from our voice boxes, we have to engage the breath. Try to speak without breathing. It is impossible. When the root of your tongue is relaxed, the breath comes in naturally and you don't have to make any concerted effort to draw breath. Whether it is the IN-Breath or OUT-Breath or a combination of both, we require the flow of air to generate speech and make a sound from our throat. Even if we are pinching ours noses when we speak, the sound is still produced by the air that is rushing through our mouth and trachea. Air and water are the main media through which sound travels. So if we wish to improve the quality, strength and timbre of our voice, we have to improve the quality of our breathing. People who sing well understand this fundamental aspect. They learn to expand their lungs, control the diaphragm and change the shape their mouths make to produce the right notes. Therefore working on the Throat Chakra entails the same involvement with our breath which will ultimately be good for our health as improved breathing means better circulation etc. This physical renewal will provide us with the moral strength to face our inner demons and old fears so that we can release them from us to enable us to express our truth.

People who developed this chakra are talented singers and orators. When the person is well-connected to a healthy Heart Chakra, the person will have great verbal ability to convince and persuade others in a compassionate way. If their Heart Chakra is not in balance such orators could use speech to deceive and manipulate for their own selfish purpose. So this shows that working on just one chakra in isolation is not conducive to the development of a holistic person. The chakras are interconnective, each having its own functions but must be properly linked and open so that all their best attributes can be manifested holistically. When this chakra is activated, the person has tremendous compassion for all sentient beings, nature and the environment.

### The Associated Element – Ether

The Collins dictionary defines *ether* the *hypothetical medium formerly believed to fill all space and to support the propagation of electromagnetic waves*. A Greek myth, as defined by the same dictionary, describes *ether* as the *upper regions of the atmosphere, clear sky or heaven*. The dictionary definition is not important but the understanding of the concept is.

As sound and hearing are not tangible objects, it is not surprising that the element associated with them and the Throat Chakra is the ether. Ether is not a solid medium and therefore it does not confine the movement of sound. Sound expresses itself in vibrations. That is why the Throat Chakra is second only to the 1st Chakra, the Muladhara Chakra to vibrate intensely. The right vibration in the right tone and key creates the perfect harmony as can be heard in beautifully orchestrated music. It also becomes a useful tool for healing. That is why Ancients have been using sound for healing purposes and so too modern technology with the use of ultra-sound. But more of this on the chapter titled, *Sounds & Mantras*.

## The Associated Colour – (Sky) Blue

The colour associated with this chakra is the 5th colour of the rainbow – blue.What more delight can we have then to look upon a warm day with green fields and blue sky? The Throat Chakra has this sense of joy and has the potential to be just as up-lifting. Just as in nature, the green fields and forests are below and the blue sky above. So too the green of the Heart Chakra is below the Sky Blue of the Throat chakra. The combination of the two in nature provides a pleasing picture and scenery. So too the combination of the Heart Chakra working in unison with the Throat Chakra is pleasing. The Heart Chakra with its expression of love and compassion grace the words that come out of the Throat Chakra with sweetness and joy.

Find something nice to say to someone. Let the words come. Let them be beautiful graceful words which will help others to smile and to open into themselves and their truth. Use the sound of your voice to bring joy to others, never pain. Always speak through the compassion and love from your heart. Make sure that you speak to yourself in the same way.

**Something To Do (10):**

Sing a song. No matter what you consider your singing voice to be. Do it in the shower if you must. But release your voice. Express yourself. Do a private Karaoke. Better still, do it under the blue sky, amongst the rolling hills. Like Maria in the *Sound of Music*, open your arms and sing at the top of your voice with a smile on your face and hear your voice as it echoes across the valley.

String up some chimes and let the wind take them to tinkle merrily in your home. Strike a Tibetan gong or bells and listen as the sound reverberates through the ether.

# CHAPTER 11

# The Sixth Chakra

*"At its best, the intuitive process brings clarity and accuracy to your
ordinary awareness and transports you into an experience of awe
about your own Divine Nature."*
Penney Peirce
*The Intuitive Way, A Guide to Living From Inner Wisdom*

The sixth chakra is called the Ajna Chakra in Sanskrit. *Ajna*
means *to know* or *to perceive*. Therefore this chakra has to do
with perception. It is the spiritual centre of knowledge, not of
the intellectual kind only but of awareness of the true self. This
knowledge is derived not through mental introspection but
through the use of insight. This is the first of the three major
chakras that are not directly associated with our five bodily
senses. However we do possess the special sense that emanates
from this chakra which has been called the sixth sense. (For some
reason that I personally don't understand, in one Tibetan
tradition, this chakra has been called the Crown Chakra which is
normally the name of the 7$^{th}$ Chakra. But this is just semantics
and we must not allow semantics to confuse our understanding.)

## The Sixth Chakra And Its Counterpart In The Physical Body

The chakra sits in the middle of our eyebrows between our two
physical eyes, hence it has been called the Third-Eye. Many
ancient traditions have represented this Third Eye in their
mythology and folklores though Hollywood-type films have
turned beings with their third-eye open into Cyclops and
monstrous creatures. One of the reasons that the unicorn is

revered is because its horn is supposed to come out of its third-eye thus signalling the fact that it is a spiritual creature. Indians in Asia acknowledge the presence of the Third-eye by putting a spot of vermillion, called the *tikka*, on their forehead. In the old days, kohl was drawn under the physical eyes to assist the physical eyes to *see spiritually* in combination with the third-eye though it has now become largely a fashion symbol.

If you were to draw a line from the space between the eyebrows right into the brain, the line will come into contact with the pituitary gland close to the hypothalamus in the brain. These two glands help to regulate the activity of most of the other endocrine glands which control the production and dissemination of hormones throughout our body. This is obviously a very important function of the brain. Our health and our moods are strongly influenced by this gland, whether we feel happy or sad or energetic or lethargic. Hormones must be kept in balance in the body for us to be in equipoise. Please don't be unduly alarmed if you are not aware of the exact locations of these glands. It does not matter as this is not a scientific or intellectual exercise. You don't have to understand human anatomy and physiology to work on a chakra as the work is on its energy rather than its physical manifestation.

Ordinarily, the chakra that has been neglected of a mention (except in Kundalini Tantric Yoga) is the *bindu chakra*. This is a minor chakra which works in unison with the Ajna Chakra. As a reference point, if you continue to draw that line from the eyebrows to the pituitary gland further back still into the brain with a slight tilt upward, you will reach the pineal gland where *bindu* is located. The bindu affects the pineal gland which lies at the roof of the thalamus and is concerned with the production of melatonin which is a very effective anti-oxidant and helps regulate our sleeping patterns. As melatonin is produced in darkness, its over-production has been suggested as the cause of SAD, Seasonal Affective Disorder (a sunlight deficiency). *Bindu* also influences the Crown or Seventh Chakra and is represented as a crescent moon in the universal OM Sanskrit character. The small dot that completes the OM Sanskrit character is supposed to be the droplet of nectar which is released from bindu when the veil of illusion or *maya* has been transcended. The reason for mentioning the bindu chakra is that there is a major pathway or *maha nadi* between the anja and bindu chakras which we will touch on again in the section on *Working Through The Chakra* in this chapter.

## Chakra Indicator

Each chakra has its shadow emotion, i.e. the opposite of the positive aspect of the chakra. So one of the indicators that a chakra is not in balance or functioning in good order is the presence of its shadow emotion – in this case, it is *confusion*. Someone who is confused emotionally is relying too much on her intellectual faculties and not enough on her intuitive faculty. Therefore she cannot achieve clarity and is thus caught in her emotional jungle, unable to see through the thicket of problems and issues. Although our five physical senses are useful for providing us with information of our body and the external world, the quality of discernment that comes from being intuitive will provide us a better perspective as it tends to look beyond the physical body and senses. Being intuitive is a reliance on an inner wisdom which takes us closer to The Divine.

The early signs of the awakening of this chakra are the imaginative and visualisation capacity of this person. She will be comfortable in dealing with abstract ideas and art-forms. This is one of the reasons why this chakra is attributed with creativity. It is linked in the concentric circle idea we mentioned in the previous chapter, to the second chakra, which also has to do with creativity but at a much more physiological level of creation (as in making babies and craftwork that are more hands-on, relying on techniques and workmanship rather than abstract inspiration.) It is the flowering of this chakra which takes a piece of writing, work or art-form from a pedestrian level to that of the genius of an artistic creation.

Of course if this chakra is open but is uncontrolled, because it is associated with the abstract and metaphysical realms, then the possibility of hallucination and the display of distorted ideas are also its potential dangers. People who attempt to raise the kundalini or serpent energy power quickly without cleansing the lower chakras are apt to be like blown-up helium balloons left afloat having been severed from their fastening or anchors.

People who suffer from severe migraines and degenerative eye-diseases may have to pay attention to what this chakra is suggesting to them.

## Posture Example

This chakra cannot be muscularly activated as it is located so far into the brain. But as its energy spreads towards the eyebrow centre, one can remind oneself of it by placing the pads of the first two fingers at the space between your eyebrows, lowering your eyes. (When Catholics make the sign of the Cross, this location is the first to be acknowledged followed by a touch to the Heart Chakra.) One of the breathing techniques of Alternate Nostril breathing use a hand position with the first two fingers in the position mentioned. It is very interesting that when you attempt to look at your own nose-tip with your eyes, the lowering of the physical eyes automatically shift the attention to the space between the eyebrow centre, the position of the Third-Eye. Try it. That is why in many of the iconic portrayals of the Buddha, he has his eyes half-closed which is what happens to the eyes when you are focusing on your nose-tip.

One of the most effective ways of opening and stimulating this chakra is the Candle-Gazing technique. Sit comfortably and place a lighted candle on the floor if you are on the floor. If you are sitting on a chair, place the candle at slightly below your eye-level so that you are not looking up to ensure that the back of your neck will be relaxed, your chin tugged in. Imagine that where the space between the eyebrows is, you do have a Third-Eye resembling a physical eye. See this opening and then look at the flame of the candle. Focus on the shape of the flame and see its different colours. Try not to blink. When your eyes are tired, close your eyes softly. See the after-image in the dark space in front of you. When you can't hold the image anymore, or if it disappears, open your eyes again and gaze at the candle flame again. Do this at least three times. You can do this whilst breathing normally. We will practise a different pattern of breathing when we come to the section of *Working Through The Chakra*

## Intuition – The Sixth Sense.
How appropriate it is that we call the sense that is derived from the Sixth Chakra – the Sixth Sense. Of course this is only semantics. We don't have to be limited by words. Words only act as pointers to the real thing and are not the things themselves, as Lao Tze tried to make us understand. Too many descriptions cloud the meaning of the Essence of Source. That is why it is stupid to quarrel over the words: *God, Allah, Jehovah* or whatever. The words point to the Essence and can only take us to a certain juncture after which we have to *experience* to understand. It is just as bad when we quarrel over words in religious texts, fighting to prove that they are the words of God, Allah or whatever. The words should act as a directional incentive for us to perceive the truth of the Divine, experientially, i.e .from our own direct experience. That means we have to do it on our own and not be reliant on any third party to tell us so. This is the ultimate journey to The Divine and learning to tune in to your intuition is the beginning of the penultimate lap of that journey. Intuition gives us insight and only with insight can we comprehend The Divine.

When we use our five senses, we are operating in the world which we apprehend through our sense of smell, taste, sight, touch or hearing. The moment we begin to enter the region of the abstract and metaphysical, we are navigating in territories that are unchartable and unverifiable by our ordinary senses. Therefore we have to use a different tool, a tool that is suited to the finer frequencies of that inner or ethereal world. This makes so much sense and yet scientific minds still dismiss the existence of this other-world simply because they are unable to collect empirical evidence but will not use the proper instrument to ascertain its existence.

Intuition is not based on logic. But as logic has been held as a yard-stick of human intelligence, what is derived in a non-logical linear fashion through the process of intuition is considered non-scientific and thus is deemed inferior or not true knowledge. This is a sad, erroneous assumption. Though science has its uses, the premises and empirical evidence demanded by science tend to circumscribe the perimeters of intuition which should have no boundaries and by its definition should remain footloose and free.

To be intuitive is to have an extra-sensory perception of consciousness. Without consciousness, we are merely animal-like, we are simply biological beings which live and die without touching the void. If we are only attached to our ego-self or OP, we remain unconscious. This is represented in yogic philosophy by the veil of illusion or *maya* because the truth of The Divine is hidden from us. The battle and current obsession with our body and our body-image arose because of this misconception, in not understanding or perceiving that we are more than just this body and mind. When we become intuitive, instead of limiting ourselves to what is observable and what is known, we are willing to be led into the unknown to perceive the mysteries of life. As intuition takes us beyond our physical boundaries, it will give us a standpoint beyond our body. Whilst engaging in this extra-sensory mode, we are able to witness our body, either in a metaphorical sense or in a real out-of-body experience. Just like any other faculty, this faculty needs to be honed and refined. This can be done through the process of introspection and meditation so that we become attuned to the rhythm and currents of the more subtle worlds.

When our 6<sup>th</sup> Chakra/Gateway has been purified and is highly developed, we gain lots of extrasensory powers, called *siddhis* in yoga. It may be that you become psychic, clairvoyant, clairaudient, etc. You might be able to levitate, have out-of-body experiences, travel astrally or whatever. Although you can enjoy the fruits of your hard work and help others with the powers you have gained or playfully manifest a parking-space, get your friend to call you, predict the winner of a race-horse or the future, these, in themselves, are *not* spiritual practices. To indulge in these powers without The Divine Connection will detract you from the True purpose of your journey. This is an important aspect to remember. Some people attain these *siddhis* and get stuck at this stage. Whether these *siddhis* were developed from a previous lifetime and are brought over into this incarnation or are developed from practices done in this lifetime is immaterial. Having these *siddhis* does not make you spiritual. It does reflect the opening of your 6<sup>th</sup> Gateway or Chakra. But if this power of gift is not used in unison with the other qualities of the other chakras, i.e. of love, compassion, insight, etc. and Divine Connection, the use of these powers could become just egoistical pursuits and goals in the interest of the lower self.

## I Have The Power To Create

The potent combination of creativity and intuitive insight can result in magnificent artistic creations. It is when we are bathed in this moment of inspiration and creation that we are our closest to The Divine. (The actual manifestation of this moment might come later, i.e. the piece of writing, music or art-form, which needs further sculpting and shaping and might involve the artist's angst and agony when she finds it a challenge to produce physically what she has intuited.) The moment of inspiration is the moment when the *chunnel* (using our earlier analogy of the Channel

Tunnel) between ourselves and The Divine is open and we are at our receptive best. At this momentous point, we too become creators and have the power to create.

Geniuses who can take us to that moment of inspiration with their work, for example in a beautiful piece of music, is helping us to experience The Divine vicariously. For in listening, we are as moved as the artist has been moved to produce it. True art is not about technical wizardry but is about expressing the infinite experience and rhythm of real life. In that exquisite moment, we are lost to our individual self and become One with the Source/Divine and all beings. It is at this juncture that we are truly Present and is in the Now.

When what we create brings joy and happiness to others, we are fulfilling the task of The Divine. That is why, as we mentioned in an earlier chapter, it is not a sin or selfish to pursue your own art because first, when you are engaged in it, you are developing your communicative power to link up with the Divine and secondly, you bring joy to others who view or experience your artistic offerings.

It is unfortunate that this power to create can also be misused and abused. This is the sad reality when egos become inflated and the propagation of the self becomes the motivator. This kind of aberration injects violence, fear and sometimes destruction into their work, generating more violence, fear and destruction in the world. Never underestimate the power of violence, fear and horror, especially those translated in visual type media. They wreak a state of unrest and insecurity. Alas we live in the world of polarities and have free will to use the gift of intuition to suit our own selfish purpose as well as for good.

## Working Through The Chakra
The side effects of working through the ajna chakra is good emotional health because the hormones will be in good balance bringing us a state of emotional equipoise where we are not

thrown asunder by our conflicting emotions. Besides a healthy diet and good exercise, a good night's sleep counts towards the way we feel. As the correct balance of melatonin is important for the quality of our sleep, working on the bindu chakra will benefit the pineal gland. Besides the Candle-Gazing asana we mentioned earlier, there is breathing technique which helps clear the *maha nadi* or main channel between the two chakras here.

Close your eyes and visualise the channel as mentioned earlier, from the space between your eyebrow to the back of your head, roundabouts to where the pineal gland is. Think of the Ancient Chinese who wear their hair in a pig-tail. The tuft of hair that is knotted arises from the back of the head roughly near the position of the internal bindu chakra, to make them remember that they are spirit manifested in a physical body. Breathe IN, move from the eyebrow centre to the back of the head. Breathe OUT, move the energy from the back of the head to the eyebrow centre.

Besides energising the two chakras here, this technique will also clear the channel. The directional movement will allow you to access your inner capacities and wisdom. Too often, we use our intellect without resource to our intuition. Working through these two chakras will help you to see with clarity, not just with your outer eyes but with your inner, hence it is called *in-sight*. By re-energising the prana and awakening the two chakras, we will awaken our intuition. This is preparing us to move onward and upward to the Seventh/Crown Chakra.

## The Associated Element – None

There is no element associated with this and the next chakra.

## The Associated Colour – Indigo

The colour associated with this chakra is the 6<sup>th</sup> colour of the rainbow – indigo. Some call the colour of this chakra Dark Blue, not dark in the sense of it being sombre but in terms of it being a deep, luxurious blue or indigo, like that of rich velvet. Think of the sky at night or a blue sapphire. This colour generates a sense of peace and tranquillity.

For our inner senses, our inner hearing and our inner sight, to be effective, we have to quieten our outer senses. Our outer senses can distract us and take us away from our true self. But if we had worked through each chakra as delineated in the last few chapters, then we can effectively use them to find our true self. As per our quotation about the mystic and poet, Kabir, when our inner hearing and inner sight are open, everything in nature, like the leaves he mentioned would become like scriptures in that they point to the written story of The Divine. We have to find ourselves before we can find The Divine. By learning how to be quiet and peaceful, not quiet and seething with suppressed anger or anxiety, we will sharpen our inner faculties. Too much talking, gossiping and bad TV will create more noise in our heads. So go and have a swim in blue water, paint a monochrome of blue or stand under the blue canopy of night-sky and allow your inner senses to flower. Be peaceful. BE.

### Something To Do (11):

Don't be afraid of going in to the inner silence where you can hone your skill at intuiting. Instead of coming from your intellect, halt your intellectual reasoning and see if you can detect something more subtle coming through. Practise on different situations and observe the outcome.

When the telephone rings, see if you can tell who might be calling you before you pick up the phone. Especially if it is someone who does not regularly call you. You will be surprised what you can intuit.

Silent meditation is an extremely useful exercise for activating this chakra. So if you have not tried it before, give it a go.

# CHAPTER 12

# The Seventh Chakra

*"To see a World in a Grain of sand/And a Heaven in a Wild Flower/*
*Hold infinity in the palm of your hand/And Eternity in an hour."*
William Blake
*Auguries of Innocence*

The seventh chakra is called the *Sahasrara Chakra* in Sanskrit. The word *Sahasrara* means *thousand* or *thousandfold*. This refers to the thousand petals of the lotus which is often used to represent this chakra. You may have already known this but in case you are not familiar, the lotus is an Eastern flower which has been used to signify a spiritual journey due to the way it makes it own physical journey to the surface of a pond. The plant starts its life in the muddy bed, the mud of the pond representing the traumas and pain that is birthed with our human incarnation or ego-self or OP. As it grows, the lotus plant is moving towards sunlight, which is symbolic of the Divine/Source or Ultimate Spiritual Goal. The plant has a long stem and has to move through murky water before it gets to the clearer water. The murkiness is symbolic of the trials, tribulations and testing we have to undergo in our life. Finally the lotus bud breaks the surface of the water and when it is exposed to sunlight, opens and flowers into a beautiful, vibrant colour. (Varieties of lotuses can be white, cream, pink or mauve. I have not seen it myself but some say that there is a blue lotus variety. At the end of each long stem is a single flower with large pads of smooth green leaves and they lie on the surface of the water very much in the manner of water-lilies as they bask in the sun.)

So as we human beings connect to the Light/ Source/The

Divine, we too begin to flower and exhibit our best colour or spiritual nature. (Incidentally each of the seven major chakras is represented by a lotus with different numbers of petals and colour. If you are interested in this, read further on it in good *Kundalini Yoga* books.) Ordinary lotus flowers do not have a thousand petals but the meaning attributed to the Seventh Chakra is that the numerous petals represent the Highest Fulfilment and Perfection possible to humanity. Iconic representations of the Buddha often show this state of Enlightenment with him wearing a gold (or otherwise) cap with a thousand studs representing the petals of the lotus. Sometimes, he is depicted with a bright halo round his head. The halo is actually the manifestation of the brilliant energy around the Sahasrara Chakra which results when this chakra is purified. This purification means that the person has reached a stage of being wholesome, holistic or holy. The halo is also used in Christian iconic figures of Jesus Christ, the Madonna and saints.

## The Seventh Chakra In The Physical Body

Although this chakra is often called the Crown Chakra and its location is cited as being on the top of our physical head, it is actually located in the boundaries of the physical and pranic body at the crown. Be aware that different schools have different inter-pretations to its exact location. Some schools suggest the back of the head for this chakra. I am apt to think that the latter is confusing the *Bindu Chakra* with the *Sahasrara Chakra*. (Some of these same schools never mention or acknowledge the existence of the *Bindu Chakra*.) (As mentioned earlier, some Tibetan schools call the chakra between the eyebrows the Crown Chakra.) Bear in mind that the perception of these chakras does not come intellec-tually but intuitively so variance in perception do occur. However it is not a damaging confusion as any work in this area will be of benefit and will activate the energies in both chakras as they are very closely located.

Many traditions and religions commemorate and protect the sacred site of the crown: Royalties wear crowns or special headdresses; the Sikhs knot their long hair over this spot by wearing a turban; the Muslims wear a *songkok* or fez; the Jews wear a skull-cap, so too does the Pope. In the old days, in some Christian sects, the monks' heads are shaved into a tonsure to indicate this spiritual gateway. This is the last of the physical gateway through which a human being can access the Divine. It is very fascinating that, though there is a good biological reason, the fontanelle of an infant is the last of its physical body to close as if the communication between The Divine and the infant is not cut off until the spirit of the baby is anchored fully in its physical embodiment. The soft part of the baby's head remains open until the skull bones close when the baby is between four to 24 months. Religious blessings are often given by placing a hand on this part of the body. Though this may be a ritualistic gesture without any specific understanding, this gesture transfers the pranic energy of the giver to the receiving chakra just as we receive the energy of The Divine through this gateway. To my mind, this shows that human beings have a much more intuitive understanding than they realise, it is just that our society with its insistence on scientific proof tend to devalue and underestimate this talent.

The chakra's part location in the brain contributes to the health of the brain and all the physical functions administered by the brain. The pineal gland is said to be the most influenced by this chakra, although as we mentioned in the previous chapter, the Ajna Chakra too shares some tasks.

## Chakra Indicator

The Masters and gurus who walk amongst us are indicators of the opening of their Crown Chakras. Remember though that no one chakra should be activated in isolation from the others. All the chakras have to be purified in order for this chakra to be activated. This means that all the positive qualities of each chakra is then combined with the positive quality of the Crown Chakra. When this chakra is open and in alignment with all the other chakras, a surge of energy runs from the base of the spine to the crown, passing through the main energy channel called the *shusumna* leading to that burst of energy called Enlightenment, where the sense of the self is unified with The Divine. Obviously my knowledge of this is only theoretical! However, I am of the notion that devoted and studious practise of deep meditation can result in small bursts of Light which are precursors to that ultimate experience of Enlightenment. These small bursts of extreme illumination which bring joy, calmness and clarity can motivate you to persevere in your spiritual endeavours. I personally experience this like a Shower of Light pouring down from above through my crown, bathing me in Golden Light. In that exquisite moment, I feel as if I am comforted and supported as if I am being taken care of and nothing could hurt me. To my chagrin, the experience for me is short-lived!

It is in these moments of being in the Light that our communication with the Divine is forged. We have passed through the gateway to apprehend The Divine. Upon our return, we are changed explicably for the good – in however small a degree. In Hinduism, the returned soul from a True Enlightenment is called a *Mahatma* or Great Soul. We gain an element of sensitivity for all sentient beings and of nature. We become more aware and more conscious, of others, of our environment and of The Divine. One of our greatest English poets, William Blake in his *Auguries of Innocence*, taught us that it is fundamentally essential that we learn to use our senses to recognise The Infinite:

> *To see a world in a grain of sand*
> *To see Heaven in a wild flower*

William Blake was considered a prophetic poet because his words have a far greater reach than our mechanistic world. But some people considered him unstable and a bit mad because he had visions which took him into different realms. Perhaps others decried him too since he was living in an age when Reason was considered of paramount importance yet Blake considered Reason to be the death of Creativity and our access to The Divine. He was my top favourite poet even when I was living in Singapore. To my joy, five years ago, after having moved away from the county in England where I had lived for more than 20 years, I moved to a coastal village only to discover that William Blake had lived in the nearby coastal village of Felpham! Of course I went along to see his thatched cottage and to the sites where he had his visions. Many of Blake's poems and verses help you to reflect inwardly so they serve as portals and will assist you in journeying towards The Divine.

## Posture Example

As the location of this chakra is on the crown of the head (or near enough), most people try to activate this by doing the Head-Stand, a posture that I do not readily recommend for people who are new to yoga or even experienced yoga practitioners who have weakened muscles or have aged physically. Of course some practitioners are perfectly capable but they too have to exercise caution and take changing factors like escalating age and variable physical conditions into account.

Though the benefits of a Head-Stand are enormous, the pressure put on weak necks and neck muscles can be dangerous and even lethal! In a properly executed Head-Stand, there should be no tension experienced in the head, neck or shoulders. But throughout my teaching years, I have seen very few students who can achieve and maintain the balance and equipoise of this posture easily, comfortably or most importantly, safely. For some people who are still attached strongly to their ego, the Head-Stand is seen as the ultimate culmination of the expert yoga practitioner, so they resort to showmanship rather than focusing on the spiritual attributes of this posture. (I too have sinned in this way when I first started out and am deeply grieved by my past vanity. Mea Culpa. Mea Culpa.)

Medical science has shown us that lack of blood to the brain has catastrophic effects. So we have to ensure that the brain is fed appropriately with nourishing blood. The main benefit of the Head-Stand is that it is an inverted posture, thus it allows blood to flow to the brain without the encumbrance of it having to go uphill as such. Second, it allows the heart to rest. The Head-Stand or any Inverted Posture achieve similar benefits. (BUT, inverted postures **should not** be done by anyone suffering from blood pressure, heart problems, vertigo, glaucoma and other eye-diseases or women who are menstruating.) An inverted posture however feeds the facial blood vessels and is thus an excellent natural face-lift! The scalp and follicles of hair are also energised by an inverted posture and will achieve the eponymous crowning glory.

So except for those types of people mentioned above, others who, if they wish to do an inverted posture, should work supervised by an experienced teacher. However, you can reap the benefits of an inverted posture through a less exacting asana which does not put any pressure on the neck and shoulder muscles.

Kneel down on all fours. Check that your arms are shoulder-width apart and that your hands are flat on the floor. Tuck your toes in so that they press into the floor. Breathe IN, push your buttock towards the ceiling and straighten your legs and your arms. For safety purpose, your palms should be flat on the floor to sustain the posture. Breathe OUT, then breathe normally. Allow your head to hang down between your arms. If possible, bring your heels down. Your neck should be free and loose and your head should feel weightless. At this point, you are achieving the closest to the Head-Stand and accruing its benefits but there is no pressure either on the head or neck muscles. Remember though that the focus is not the binding physical form but on spiritual boundlessness!

## Sense Of Cosmic Consciousness.

If Cosmic Consciousness can be called a sense, then it is a transcendent sense as it is not an awareness of the empirical realm. This is Cosmic Consciousness where you are in tune with The Divine. Once you have passed through the seventh gateway of your body, you are beyond the strictures of the mental and physical bodies. This is true freedom. To know The Divine is to understand your own Divinity and to tap into the power of The Divine. When you view reality, the falsity and transient nature of this world become evident. You are no longer fooled by its polarities and transitory attractions. Life then takes on a deeper meaning as you separate the wheat from the chaff.

As compassion is a key aspect of your evolvement, the moment you establish a link with The Divine, you bring back the peace and joy of The Divine into the world and you act with compassion. This is the key to freedom because you can still operate in this world without becoming attached to your actions, as in expecting returns. You become unattached or detached from the fruits of what you reap. Even in loving others, we can be attached by our expectation for them to love us in return or we lay claim to ownership of them. If we function on the level of the biological animal, the sense of ownership of our family and propagating our species is huge. We have to move away from this attachment in order for us and members of our family to live their Life's Purpose. Having the sense of cosmic consciousness, we become aware that we are part of all sentient beings and not to just a specific few who happened to be in our group of family or friends. So our behaviour and attitude transcends belonging, race, colour or creed. This is non-attachment at its most sublime.

## I Am A Spirit Having A Physical Experience

The activation and opening of the sixth and seventh gateways invariably expose you to the more subtle realms so that you are more au fait about how things operate and work at this level. Through the development of your intuitive and cosmic consciousness prowess, you start to learn to navigate in an ethereal landscape which may have so far eluded you or you may not have been able to grasp. You will soon learn that the restriction your mind had imposed on you through fear of the unknown is a false restriction and this becomes no longer binding. You are capable of moving out of the confined physicality of your body, initially in an abstract intuitive way then eventually in a significant manner in what is generally termed an out-of-body experience. Science claimed that the latter is a psychological aberration. But those who can command their soul to wander away from the space of their physical bodies know that this is not an aberration but a release from a physical prison. Imagine that you grow up living in an enclosure, high walls all around you. All the people in that enclosure had also grown up with the belief that there is no life outside the walls. People live and die within those walls. No one could even consider or think of trying to get beyond the walls. But one day, one plucky person tried to get beyond the walls. To her astonishment, she discovered that the gates have never been locked and she could simply walk through, out of the prison. This is the same with our lives. We have been so used to living in our bodies, which act like our enclosure or prison. Because the body, like the walls, are solid, no one considers or thinks that there might be a way of going beyond it. But there is. As soon as you apprehend The Divine, you learn the true nature of things. The Dalai Lama, in his *Book Of Daily Meditations*, said, "*Although space seems empty, once you develop the energies, you can control it. When that happens, you can look right through solid things and walk in empty space as if it were solid.*"

You don't have to take any of this on board. The experience is yours to discover in your own time if you have the inclination. But it is when you are able to stand away from your physical form to observe your own body is when you arrive at your greatest realisation that you are indeed Spirit having a Physical Experience. No one has to tell you this. This is not based on faith but your own experience. Only, like sky-diving, you first have to jump out of an aeroplane at 12,000 feet into thin air to experience the wonder of flight. No one can correctly describe the intensity of that feeling when there is no ground to support you and yet somehow you know yourself to be supported and safe and filled with exquisite joy. Yes, it is frightening to be in a plane with its open doorway as it climbs up higher and higher and you see the land falling away from you. The transcendental experience can have a similar unnerving moment but the exhilaration of your discovery and connection to The Divine will be so inspiring that you will want to go through it again and again!

I might be shot for this. But when the Christians say that man is made in God's image, they understand it to be that God looks like a human being, as opposed to say, an animal or a Martian. My understanding of that quotation is that yes, we are made in God's image but it is not about the human image. God is Spirit and so are we.

## Working Through The Chakra
The most effective method for you to arrive at the gateway where you can comprehend The Divine is through meditation. Different schools and traditions have different techniques. You can find one to suit you at the stage you are at and you can move on to different techniques when you are more confident, if you so wish. Meditation is very much an over-used word that can mean all sorts of things to all sorts of people. Some people think that positive visualisation is meditation. It is not. It may be a step towards controlling your thoughts but it is not meditation. The yogis and Masters of old devised ways for us in which we can

hone our skills to apprehend the subtler dimensions and fine-tune our receptivity to The Divine. Meditation is a method of opening your *chunnel* to the Divine. If you are praying, generally, the direction of flow is from you to The Divine, you expressing what it is you need from The Divine. The Divine does not pray back at you! But when you meditate, the direction of flow and communication is two-way, you pause your thoughts to listen to what The Divine is also saying to you. I think this aspect is crucial if we wish to receive Divine inspiration and intercession for the problems in our lives. If you tell your problems to your human friend but never stop to listen to her advice, you won't make any progress. It is the same if you spend all your time talking to The Divine without listening. The key is in the listening.

Although seated mediation is the ultimate posture which will bring about stillness and calm, other forms of meditation can lead you to prepare the body and mind for it. Meditation can include active or moving mediation. That is why in Zen meditation, Hatha Yoga and Tai Chi and other such practices, the physical movements have been called Meditation-In-Action. The essential characteristic of meditation is that one must apply one's complete awareness to it, whether it is in performing a posture, on one's breath, walking or sitting. Therefore if one is mindful when one is carrying out a task, when your mind is in the Present watching where you put your feet when you walk, how you wash your dishes, how you cut the vegetables, these simple practices of mindfulness is meditation-in-action. So your everyday activities can be practises of mindfulness, cooking for the family, cleaning the house, bathing the baby, doing your office-work, gardening etc.

In yoga, the whole system of Hatha Yoga is designed not for physical prowess or even good health but for the ability to put your body in a position where it is comfortable for meditation. In seated meditation, the spine is normally held at a comfortable but straight position because the main energy channel can be kept open. *Padmasana* or the full Lotus Posture was not designed for anyone to show how supple they can be by sitting cross-legged. If the posture is held properly, the crossed legs form a sturdy triangular base so that the meditator is kept upright and firm so that when the meditator starts to relax or fall asleep, she won't topple over. The crossing of the legs on top of each other meant that the heels are into the groin to activate the minor chakras that are in the groin area. Usually the hands are held in a *mudra* or seal position or gestures to activate particular currents of energy. So every position has a significance. All the dynamic yoga asanas were designed and preformed to keep your body supple and to release the tension in muscles and joints to prepare the body to sit in comfort in seated meditation for long periods. All the other purposes which we attribute to asanas, ie to keep our body toned, making it healthy, losing weight etc are by-products, not the goal.

But having said that, if getting into Lotus Position means that you are in pain, your mind will be directed to that pain and so the intent and integrity of that posture is lost. In this instance it is far better to sit in an Easy or Tailor Pose when the legs are loosely folded to achieve the sturdy triangular base but does not cause you discomfort or pain. If necessary, you can also sit on a chair to be in comfort so that you can be in true meditation though it is advisable to keep your back away from the chair so that the energy flow is not restricted. In the extreme scenario when you have to lie down to meditate as when you are ill, you can still attempt it though you are very likely to fall asleep as mediation takes you into the restful Alpha state.

Our normal brain wave activity is measured in waves. When we are functioning in our daily life, we are operating at Beta Level which is the highest number of wave-undulation per second. The next level is the Alpha Level which is our relaxed and creative level. Generally we experience this for a few minutes before dropping off to sleep at the Theta and Delta levels. Artists, musicians, poets and writers get their inspirational ideas whilst in this Alpha state. This is also our best frequency to tune in to the frequency of The Divine – at this Alpha Level. That is why all meditation techniques will attempt to create the right conditions for you to access this frequency but without falling asleep. That's why a seated posture is important.

In the beginning of this book, we mentioned that it is possible to right some wrongs that we may have done in the past. This can be done through meditation. Science establishes time as a linear process for ease of function. In actuality time exists in a holographic way in that Present, Past and Future can all be accessed Now. If this concept gives you a headache or makes you roll your eyes up in total disbelief, don't worry. You don't have to take it on board. However, when your 6th and 7th Chakras are open, the concept won't seem as crazy.

But let us assume that though you can set aside your rational objection and you are happy to work on past issues. Get into a meditative mode and revisit that past incident where perhaps someone has been hurt by your words or action. Use The Divine Energy that you now possess and send it to the person you were and the person you were involved in. Replay the situation in your Mind's Eye but this time let it end with more positive consequences. See the other person smiling from your generous and kind input. Forgive yourself and return to the present. If it is a very strong issue, you may have to do this several times. If you are still in touch with this person, notice the new energy between you two the next time you meet even if the person did not know what you have done. Energy transcends linear time. The meditative process is like a Clearing House, it gets rid of lots of old stuff to make way for the new.

## The Associated Element – None
Like the previous chakra, there is no element associated with this.

## The Associated Colour – Violet and The Rainbow

Violet is the 7$^{th}$ colour of the rainbow and completes the spectrum of the rainbow colours. See it as a rich mix of red and blue, like the velvet worn by Royals. But unlike colour in a fabric, this colour is alive and pulsing with energy, mingling with the colours of the chakras below it. Think of sunshine and summer violet flowers bursting with brightness and glory.

So celebrate the fact that you have a rainbow in you. When all your chakras are purified and cleansed, their colours will glow with vibrancy and beauty. This is the beauty that permeates your skin, whether your skin is young and taut or old and wrinkled. This is beauty that is beyond skin and superficiality. Skin that is artificially pulled tight through poison and surgery will not have this special translucency. It will appear dead and inert. That is why people who have had plastic surgery done need lots of make-up to disguise this fact. But skin nourished by our inner glow and Divine Energy will be graced by vitality and will look alive. If you have the good fortune to be in the presence of a Master, Guru or Enlightened Sage, observe what good vibes you get from them and observe how they glow even if they might be physically old and wrinkled. This is true beauty that never dies. Why reach for artifice when you can have the Real Thing? Remember that your True Beauty can never be erased by age nor infirmity.

Do you remember the lighted barber pole located at the shop-front of an old-fashioned barber? The pole is in white and red if I am not mistaken. The analogy I would like to use here is the way the colours swirl and twist within the pole. But if you have not seen one, don't worry. What you want to imagine is that all the colours of your seven chakras are not static. They are pulsating with energy and they swirl around in constant movement, sending sparks of light around your body. In science, experiments have been carried out where the colours of the rainbow are spun at great speed and the result of this is White Light. So it is safe to say that White Light is actually composed of all the beautiful colours of the rainbow. That is why Divine Light descending from above is often depicted as White Light though some might view it as Golden.

When all your seven chakras are purified, you have also purified your *koshas* or sheaths, the lampshades which we spoke about earlier in Chapter 4, which hide your Inner Light. Cleansing the chakras refine the various sheaths to make them more translucent so that the Divine Light that you receive can be combined with your Inner Light to shine from every pore of your skin.

Imagine that your Crown Centre is open and you are under a shower of White Light! This is when you are receiving the Divine Energy through your uppermost gateway. Most religious traditions have mentioned the receiving of this Light, some called it The Spirit, some call it Grace. By whatever name you know it, open yourself to receive.

When the Great Flood subsided, God promised Noah that He would never cause such a flood again. To make good His Promise, he sent the rainbow. When you see a rainbow appear in the sky, it is a time for smiles and rejoicing. Celebrate the rainbow. Remember that the beautiful rainbow with all its resplendent colours is also within you and without.

---

**Something To Do (12):**

Search for rainbows everywhere. They might not always be whole or large rainbows in the sky. See them in the dewdrops on blades of grass, in drops of water, in the shimmering waves, refracted in glass, in a flame. Even on your skin or in a spot of grease. Paint or draw a rainbow. Let the rainbow remind you of the rainbow within. Celebrate your Divinity and the glory of The Divine. Have a go singing my song, *Rainbows Everywhere* which is at the end of the last chapter to remind you of its symbolism.

---

# CHAPTER 13

# SOUND AND MANTRA

*"The chanting human voice, in fact, is the world's oldest musical instrument. Every culture and civilisation has recognised its magical power."*

*Healing Mantras*, Thomas Ashley-Farrand

In *Genesis*, in the Christian Bible, it is said, *"In the beginning was the Word and the Word was God."* In the ancient Sanskrit texts of the Vedas, some 3000 years before the Bible was written, a similar line says, *"In the beginning was the Sound and the Sound was OM."* I am sure you can agree that the Word mentioned in the Bible was the Spoken Word rather than the Written Word. After all, the Bible was not written until hundreds of years after Jesus Christ had ascended into Heaven, before printing became commonplace. In another translation of the Vedic quotation, it is said, *"In the beginning was the Vibration and the Vibration was OM."* Of course there cannot be sound if there is no vibration of the sound. This vibration of OM is supposed to be the most primeval of vibrations and sound. Even when you listen as the wind blows through your chimney, you can hear this OM hum coursing through your house. If you listen carefully, particularly with your inner ears as accentuated by the 6th chakra, you can hear this wondrous hum that is part of the essence of our everyday life. It is only the yogis who have named it OM as it is the closest word that reflects its sound but its ownership is not particular and is universal as it is part of the Great Cosmos which belongs to everybody.

The word *Om* is in Sanskrit. Unlike English and many languages which are meaning-based, Sanskrit is sound-based, i.e phonetic. All Sanskrit vowels and diphthongs are vibrational sounds, not letters to be written but sounds to be uttered. This aspect is particularly significant when it comes to Sanskrit chanting. Sanskrit writing is called *Devanagari* script. *Deva* being a god, so Devanagari is the language of the gods (thereby is considered a Celestial Language.)

Whatever religious tradition we come from, sound has been used as a key factor in our praise of The Divine. It is expressed with our human voice in salutations, supplications, prayer, songs of praise and chanting. Dramatic chants have been attributed to black magic practitioners, witches and wizards, some of them abusing their power but more than not, when we think of chants, we think of its positive usage and its energising devotional effects. Lately we have come to associate chanting with Eastern practises, in yogic and Buddhistic chants. Yet the Christian tradition too has a long history of using chants, the most well-known and one of the most beautiful, being the Gregorian chant. In the old practice of conducting mass, chants were sung in Latin and they used to resonate across the vaulted spaces of our churches and cathedrals. So chants are universal, not confined to any particular race or creed.

In combination with our human voice, most of these chants are accompanied by bells, gongs, drums or blowing of conch shells. Although musical instruments might accompany a chant, the main musical instrument used is the human voice.

The public celebration of The Divine in churches, temples or mosques uses sound to gather the people, as in a muezzin calling everyone to prayer or the church bells ringing to remind people to pray or come to church. Sounds is also used as a means to hold the attention of the celebrant. This is the sense associated with our 5th and 6th gateways to the Divine, the chakras which have to do with the production of sound and the faculty of listening to those sounds. Often, our sense of smell is also engaged through the use of incense, joss sticks, scented wood and candles or fresh flowers meaning that our 1st gateway is also involved. In fact all of our senses are involved in some way or another. The Heart Centre or 4th gateway is the means of devotion through which we can express our love for The Divine. But it is the use of sound, with communal prayers and hymns which produces cohesion in a religious community, bringing disparate people together, sharing one voice.

## Chanting Mantras For Calming Down

When you are upset, you are in a highly emotionally charged state. Therefore to move you from that state to one of calm, spiritual disciplines tend to use words that are non-emotive. The words themselves vary, according to the spiritual disciplines, they can be devotional words naming the relevant deities or saints or they could be seed words that have special magical powers. To keep pace with the counting, rhythm and beat of the special words or mantra, the Catholics use the rosary, the Muslims, Hindus and Buddhists use prayer beads or mala. Not dissimilar really. Whether it is the Hail Mary or a mantra, the essence of the practice is that the words have to be repeated again and again to reinforce its potency. The word mantra has now been accepted into the English Language and is used to express this idea of repetition. Therefore any devotional word-repetition is considered a mantra. However, the original meaning of this word means that it is an encrypted Sansksrit word or words which has/have an encoded power within them. Swami Vishnu Devananda, in his book, *Meditation and Mantras*, said, "*A mantra is mystical energy encased in a sound structure.*" Repeating a mantra again and again is actually called *japa* in Sanskrit. The Sanskrit term *mantra* is made up of two words, *man*, meaning to *think* (which forms the word, *manas*, meaning *mind*.) *Tra* is from the word *trai*, meaning *to protect* or *free*, as in *to free from the phenomenal world*. Swami Devananda's guru, Swami Sivananda said that, "*A mantra generates the creative force and bestows eternal bliss. A mantra when constantly repeated awakens the consciousness.*"

In Sanskrit mantra repetition, it is recommended that a mantra be repeated 108 times for it to be really effective. Swami Jnaneshvara Bharati cites several reasons why 108 beads are used. Not all the reasons are covered here. One possible reason, he said, is that 9 and 12 are spiritual numbers so 9 times 12 equals 108. There are also 12 planets and 9 houses in astrology. In some schools, 1 represents God/The Divine, 0 stand for emptiness or completeness in spiritual practise, 8 for infinity. (The Chinese too ascribe to this.) In yoga, it is said that there are 108 energy inter-sections in the subtle body called *marmas* or *marmasthanas*. For ease of counting the repetitions, the *mala* was produced with 108 beads which were originally fashioned out of lotus roots and threaded in a circle with a main larger tasselled bead, called the *meru*, to signify the beginning and end of the cycle. The idea is not to cross this *meru*. It is fascinating that the Catholic Rosary has 54 beads, exactly half the number of beads of a mala. For further ease a *japa mala*, has half the number in a rosary with 27 beads which makes it more convenient to carry around.

Therefore the act of repeating a mantra will help to reduce the fluctuations of the brain waves in the brain, taking you from beta waves level down to alpha which is a more restful state in the brain and also the most creative. Therefore repetition of mantras is one of the key techniques in meditation.

Try it. If you are caught in a fit of anger, take yourself to somewhere where you can be undisturbed. Even if you can't go somewhere undisturbed and are at your desk, for instance, the technique will still work. Let us pick two or more words that will be like a boat to take you to calmer waters. If you are a Christian, you could use a Christian prayer, like Hail Mary full of grace. Or you could use a yogic one, *Om Bhagavate Vasu Devaya*. (This mantra asks for assistance to put you in touch with The Divine.) Repeat the words. Until you find your mind settling down, then your feelings, then your body. The repetition has a soporific effect allowing any tension within your body or mind to dissolve away.

## Chanting Mantras To Aid A Broken Spirit

In yogic philosophy, a repetitive word or mantra has other significance. A mantra is not just a meaningless repitition but is a technique of protection, protecting you from the primeval reaction of your own body and mind so that you steer clear of unbridaled and reactive emotions. The mantra will jump-start your spiritual batteries. When you have those few minutes of calm, your Intuitive Self will kick in and your connection with The Divine is forged. Henceforth whatever decision you take will be better informed rather than that which is taken when your emotions are raw and operating from the Ego-Self/OP.

Mantra repetition helps to revitalise both the physical body and the subtler body. It is usually done with the breath so mantra practice will improve the quality of your breath and more importantly, the prana. Therefore, regular mantra practise mends and heal not only a broken heart, but also a broken body and broken mind but a broken spirit.

We know what it is like when we have to do a difficult task ourselves. For instance, if a tree has fallen over your drive and you don't have a saw to cut the tree into smaller portions and you had to move it yourself, you will struggle, sweat and pant. If a neighbour(s) came round to help you, you can lift the tree much quicker. So when you are struggling with your inner demons, why not call upon friends to help you? They might be Earthly Friends or they might be Beyond-Earthly or as I call them, My-Friends-Upstairs. Why struggle on your own? Call on your spiritual neighbours and friends: saints, deities, angels and The Divine to help you lift yourself from the burden of your emotions and thoughts. This is mantra used as an invocation where you call upon the names of Blessed Beings to help you. Hail Mary! Mother of God! Blessed Jesus! Ya, Allah! Laksmi, Shiva, Krisha, Yahweh, Kwan Yin. Don't be too shy to call for help. How effective you are in your telephone line to *Upstairs* is dependent on how well your *chunnel* is open, the tunnel that has been cleared by clearing all the obstructions in your various gateways. Reciting a mantra acts like the TBM, Tunnel Boring Machine to The Divine, because it clears the obstructions.

## Chanting Mantras For Healing

Except for a vacuum, sound travels through the atmosphere. To contribute to the world's positive energy, make sure that whatever sound you make is pleasing to the atmosphere. Pleasant sounds are very good mood setters. That is why music has been used for millenniums to enhance the mood of romantic love and desire. The right music can create a relaxing mood. Think of the sound of cowbells twinkling gently in the Swiss Alps echoing across the mountains and valleys. Gentle pleasing sounds are restful and can be healing for the spirit. That is why a beautifully composed piece of music with its harmony of instruments used in the correct key can be so soothing. Studies are being made to discover the connection of music to healing. Some people have experimented by playing music and talking to plants to help them to grow better. Discordant and harsh sounds have the opposite effect hence people living in troubled families and cities with the constant blaring of traffic and white noise are much more wound-up thus lowering the level of their immunity and are more prone to illnesses than those living in happier homes or the country-side.

Sound travels through water as well, and since our body is made up of a large percentage of water, sound is a useful tool for healing our physical body as well, either on its own or in combination with the use of herbs and medicine. That is why ancients have been using sound for healing purposes, the medicine man chanting and invoking the benevolent spirits, the healer mumbling or chanting sacred words. Sometimes they might brandish and wave about with wands or rattles and even get into some kind of dance and jig but the main thrust is the sound they make. In our more sophisticated time, the pitch of sound has been refined into an ultra-sonic level to aid in the healing process. Yet before this modern discovery and invention, this same scientific-minded person might have poohed-poohed the fact that sound can indeed heal. The yogis have known it for centuries!

Mantras used specifically for healing are encrypted with the right vibrations by our Past Spiritual Explorers to activate the healing capacities of your body. Chanting these mantras will help your heart-beat to slow down, your blood pressure to be reduced and your muscles start to relax. Mantras heal by loosening the grip of pain and sorrow that are held within the body. Experts on mantras will provide you with the appropriate mantras for specific conditions. Thomas Ashley-Farrand, the writer of *Healing Mantras* cites a general healing mantra:

*Om Sri Dhanvantre Namaha*
*Salutations to the being and power of the Celestial Physician.*

This mantra can be used for any condition or situation that requires healing. Healing can come in all sorts of ways. In Asia, it is the practise of good home-makers to spoon love and joy into the meals they cook so that all those who eat the food you cook will be imbibed with love and joy. The more spiritual home-makers also inject the food with healing properties by chanting the above mantra whilst cooking so that people who eat their food will be healed from their sadness, loneliness or pain. (Incidentally, it is through this manner that cooking a meal can become a spiritual exercise.)

For deep healing , read about the *Maharityunjaya Mantra* in the section on *Heal The World, Chant*!

## Sanskrit Mantras In Yogic Tradition

In yogic tradition, a Sanskrit mantra is not received intellectually but is perceived while in a mystical state. Since the Gurus and Masters perceived these mantras whilst they are in a state of Sublime Consciousness, it means that when users recite the mantra, the mantra has the power to induce and take them to that state of Sublime Consciousness. The mantra is passed from Master to Pupil orally, not written. In the same way that the pitch and wave-length in an Ultra-Sound has been modulated for optimum performance in healing, the Masters taught that the organs of speech or production of sound, i.e. the tongue, throat and mouth, etc., can be shaped and modulated to evoke the healing qualities of the mantra. For example, the universal sound of OM can be broken into three parts to guide and manipulate the vibration and sound into the different areas of the mouth and throat to generate its strongest power and energy. OM is thus divided into A-U-M. When enunciating A (as in fA-ther), the mouth is open so the sound starts in the cavity of the mouth. As it continues into U, (as in Umbrella) the mouth is slightly closed and the vibration is directed to the roof of the mouth. Proceeding to the M part (as when we hum), the mouth is completely closed and the sound is taken right to the back of the throat. Each part of the mantra triggers off minor chakras in the various areas to activate their latent power. This is the way in which mantras are articulated and sounded to help in the healing process.

There are many good books of examples of mantra and one that comes with a useful CD to get the pronunciation correct is one quoted at the top of this chapter by Thomas Ashely-Farrand. There are mantras that are targeted for particular purposes. Mantras also heal by creating the right ambience for healing to take place. Chanting a particular targeted mantra can expose you to the right condition or professional help that might be required for healing to occur. Mantras are not used in place of medical assistance or intervention but are used in harmony with it. Healing can be physical, emotional and psychological.

## Different Types Of Mantras
When we invoke the name of a deity in a mantra, calling upon Shiva or Laksmi, Jesus or Mary, or Mohammed, the mantra is

called a Deity Mantra. This is a direct telephone call to the deity to come and provide succour. The characteristic of a mantra is that it turns the mind towards concentration on The Divine. The process will release energy into the chakras. Most of these mantras tend to be preceded by the universal vibration, *Om* and followed by seed or *bija* mantras. These seed sounds have no exact meanings in that they are the base sounds which are then attached to other mantras like the deity mantras although they have a significant purpose, for example, the seed sound, *shrim*, is used if you want abundance and *klim* is used to attract. Sometimes the two seed sounds are put together in a mantra to maximise their effect. Thomas Ashley-Farrand, aka Namadeva, suggests that we repeat each seed mantra at least twice for its effect to take place. Other yogis sometimes suggest a minimum of three repetitions. Then there are abstract or *nirguna* mantras which are designed to set up powerful vibrations within the body that will help you connect instantly with The Divine. Many of these are high-octane types, passed on from guru to pupil. A bit like Instant-Fix to Enlightenment. Some mantras are far too powerful for us mere mortals to mishandle, like playing carelessly with nuclear energy. Our etheric body must be prepared to receive such intensity of power-charge. You could be fried-roasted by its lightning-force! So be cautious. Work on the safe ones and be guided by experienced teachers to take you through to the more esoteric ones. The study of mantra is huge and can encompass several books so what we are discussing here is only a pointer to whet your appetite for more.

## Sanskrit Seed Mantras To Unlock The Seven Gateways

If you wish to go through a physical door which is locked, you obviously need the appropriate key. It is not much good if you have a Chubb lock and you try to open it with a padlock key. Logically, it makes sense that there are different keys for different types of doorways. For example, Aladdin opened the door to his cave with his magic words, *Open Sesame*. Lots of modern doors to high-security places are opened with numerical codes and/or thumb-print identification. Some companies are trying to develop doors which can only be opened by a light-examination of the pupils of a person's eye to prove his identity. The more the need for security, the more complex the method of opening that particular door has to be to prevent fraud or wrongful entry. So too it is with etheric doorways.

First and foremost, the etheric doorways are not physical and are not visible to the physical eye. This provides the first challenge – the doorways have to be visualised and seen with the inner eye. Secondly, the key that is to be used for the etheric doorway is also an abstraction rather than a solid key which you can hold in your hand. But the cave of The Divine Consciousness is a treasure-house of valuables and jewels which will make us exceedingly joyous in our day-to-day life so we have to persevere. So, to go through the seven etheric gateways of our body into the cave of The Divine, we must use the right etheric key. Each of the seven major chakras has its own *key or Bija* or Seed Mantra. A Seed Mantra, is as the word suggests, the basic component of a mantra that has the first unlocking mechanism to open the gateway of a chakra. However, it can be used on its own in its entirety or can be used in combination with other components of a mantra which has the effect of a set of combination-numbers that opens a safe. For instance, OM, is the Seed Mantra of the 6th Chakra. As this Seed Mantra has a Cosmic quality and is considered a principle of unity, it tends to be used with other combination of mantras which invoke the Universal, *Om Shanti, Om Namah Shivaya, Om Dum Durgayei Namaha, Om Mani Padme Hung.*

In using a physical key, we turn the key in the lock. To use an etheric key, we allow our mind to focus on the corresponding chakra and visualise its corresponding colour. Then repeat the appropriate mantra at least three times to activate the lock. Here are the keys or Seed Mantras for each of the gateway of your body to unlock it so that you can go through to apprehend The Divine:

LAM – 1st Chakra
VAM – 2nd Chakra
RAM – 3rd Chakra
YAM – 4th Chakra
HAM – 5th Chakra
OM  – 6th Chakra
OM  – 7th Chakra

Generally, as a kind of loose yard-stick, the Seed Mantra you find difficult to work with points to the fact that its corresponding chakra is out of kilter and is the one you really need to work on. If you find any giving you problems, go back into the appropriate chapters to remind yourself of the issues that that particular chakra is attached to. Then go into yourself to see what emotional situations have happened in your past to shackle you to these issues. For instance, if your desire for sex had led you astray previously or caused hurt to someone, cleanse and purify the 2nd Chakra by chanting the seed mantra, *VAM* repeatedly. Or, if currently, you feel yourself aroused very often and you are tempted to engage in indiscriminate or casual sex, chant the mantra to help you bring the chakra into balance so that the sexual energy can be transmuted into a creative energy. With love and compassion, kindly and gently release its hold on you.

## Mantra practice

Mantra practice is your key to unlock the gate into the subtler kingdom. Synchronising mantra repetition with the breath, the practice is your daily forging to The Divine Energy. It is a reminder to yourself that you are not just this body and mind but you are something more. Making your connection with The Divine also means that you are never alone, never without Divine Assistance. Do this first thing in the morning and last thing at night – and anytime in-between when you have a moment to spare.

First thing in the morning, offer your day to The Divine. Be glad that you are still alive on this Earth to experience The Divine through The Divine's manifested works as in nature. Realise that you are the author of your day, you can make it into the kind of day you want. Send blessings to people you know, people you don't know, all the animals and living things in the world. Be ready to see the Divine expressed in the world about you and in the people you meet. At the end of the day, be thankful for the things you have had and experienced and the people who had come across to teach you something. Use your prayer or mantra to tune in and hold on to The Divine frequency. You don't have to go to a church or temple to do this. You can do this wherever you are. The Divine is everywhere, not confined to bricks and mortar.

Mantras can be sounded out loud. Or they can be chanted softly like a whisper. Then finally sound it only in your head. Feel the difference. Feel what it is doing to your body. Feel what it s doing in your mind. If you are tuned into the appropriate frequency, you can actually feel the mantra vibrating throughout your body and mind even if you are chanting the mantra silently. But don't take my word for it, find it out for yourself. This is your own voyage of discovery. Go for it! (It is said that Adepts, Gurus and Masters can pick up the vibrational-energy of a mantra that is being recited by another person even when the person is chanting silently and can know what mantra it is.)

## Mantras For Every Occasion

It is said that there is a mantra for every occasion! One to connect to the Spirit, one for abundance, one for good health, wealth, romance, etc. etc. There are many published books and CDs on the subject. Find a book to suit you.

In all the various practises, it is encouraged that for effectiveness, you stay with one mantra for 40 days. For some reason, this is the magical number. It has something to do with the config-uration of numbers and its properties. You may recall that Jesus Christ went into the desert for 40 days. The rain that fell on Noah and his Ark went on for 40 days. Try it yourself. Choose a mantra that is going to help you to deal with the present issue you are struggling with in your life.

Repeating a mantra for 40 days means that the mantra is ingrained into you and you can call on it when you need the appropriate one. I find it useful to write the mantra down in a Mantra Journal with its meaning in English and the date I started working with it and write down the date when the 40 days is up. There are some schools which specify the exact number of times a mantra must be repeated for it to be properly effective, for example, 125,000 times! But generally, if you repeat a mantra for ten minutes each day, it will be a good start. If you like, you can use a *mala* to help in the counting. Completing one mala will mean you have done 108 repititions.

I would like to share with you how much mantras have worked for me! If I questioned their efficacy before, I certainly did not during the most difficult time of my life. I'm now so convinced of their power that I want everyone to benefit from them as I have benefited from them. Four years ago, in my middle-age, I went through a horrific divorce from my English husband. Although he was a wealthy man and we were living in a very big house with a life-style to match, he offered me £20,000 as a settlement, no alimony and no home, claiming that he owned nothing. Everything I thought we owned had been signed over to his children from his first wife. I had given up my native homeland for him and we were married and had been together for nearly 25 years. Since I was working in his several businesses, the divorce also meant that I had no job and, worse, no income. I discovered that a good-paying job was scarce for a middle-aged woman especially one who had no credentials for working in the field of Marketing and PR in the UK and outside her husband's business. Imagine my predicament! Even through that horror, my love for him triumphed and I opted out of going to trial for fear of washing our dirty linen in public and for fear of him being incarcerated for his actions. To cut a very long and tortured story short, eventually my solicitors managed to wrest a modest home and a pension from him for me. Fortunately, during our marriage, I had the foresight to do a post-graduate degree in Creative Writing, trained to be a yoga teacher and worked on my books on top of the work I had to do for my husband plus cook him three meals a day as his office was in the grounds of our home. The greatest pain I felt was one of a sense of having been betrayed by someone I had loved and trusted.

During that challenging period, I really revved up on my mantra chanting. To ask for the obstacles to be removed from my path, I chanted *Om Gum Ganapatayei Namaha*. I chanted the mantra *Om Shrim Maha Laksmiyei Swaha* for Abundance. Mind you, it took several thousand repetitions before their effect finally kicked in! But kicked in, they did. Then the work offers came. I was offered many teaching assignments and talk engagements; my articles and short stories were accepted for publication. Then this publisher accepted this book! Even my tax code changed for me to benefit more from my meagre income and I even had a tax rebate! I even had a free holiday to the Caribbean as a birthday present from a long-term friend who paid for me to attend her son's wedding! And to cap all that, the Singapore Government granted me a five-year permit to return to Singapore to be with my family so that I don't have to live in England alone. I used *Om Namo Bhagavate Vasudevaya* and *Namyoho Renge Kyo* (a Japanese Buddhist mantra )to focus on my highest spiritual aspirations in order that I do not allow anger and hurt to corrode me into revenge. I chanted *Om Mani Padme Hung* (Tibetan Buddhist mantra) to develop compassion in my Heart Chakra so that I can release the pain my Ex inflicted on me with his words and actions, then finally to forgive him for making money his priority rather than love. Over and above all the other mantras, I chanted the Gayatri Mantra every single day to take me through the roughest days of living in a B& B until I had my own home.

## A Powerful, Universal Mantra –The Gayatri Mantra

The mantras of all Sanskrit mantras is the *Gayatri Mantra* which is a very long mantra but is worth learning as it is a powerful, universal mantra which will help you to reap huge benefits through the transformation of your body and mind. The mantra is the 16th sutra or aphorism from the Rig Veda, one of the four books of the ancient Vedas. The Gayatri Mantra invokes the Goddess Gayatri Devi who is a patron of the Arts and is a skilled composer, poet and musician. She is attributed as having given mankind the Four Vedas. Rishis i.e. wise men of India, arranged the 14 words of the Gayatri Mantra in a special order to convey meaning and to generate specific power through their utterance and to inspire wisdom. This is considered the short form or short version:

*Aum Bhur Bhuvah Swah Tat Savitur Varenyam*
*Bhargo Devasya Dhimahi Dhiyo Yo Nah Prachodayat*

Don't worry about the individual meanings of the words as the essence of it is more important. (However when you become a serious student of mantras, as taught by a proper guru, each Sanskrit word carries a potent *mantra shakti* or power therefore must be enunciated properly to evoke its potency.) For our uninitiated, general purpose, we will dwell on its meaning. The usual English translation of the mantra goes like this:

*Oh, God, Thou art the Giver of Life, the remover of pain and sorrow,*
*The bestower of happiness, O creator of the Universe,*
*May we receive thy Supreme sin-destroying Light,*
*May Thou guide our intellect in the right direction*

The mantra is a meditation on Spiritual Light, *savitur*, meaning the quality of *Light* which illuminates all the spheres of Light. These spheres of Light are in the region where the Divine Frequency is located. The spheres or *lokas* could be likened to the *house of many mansions* that Jesus spoke about in The Bible. The mantra invokes the vibrational sound of each of the sphere thereby bringing Divine Light into our physical body. This is the Light that shines out from the faces of the Enlightened Ones, Gurus and Masters, the light of everlasting beauty and purity that no physical deterioration can damage. Even if we do not reach this extreme High State, chanting this mantra will energise the prana in degrees in our body, giving us good health, which in turn will generate a wonderful glow from within thus lightening the coarseness of our physical body. It will also cast Divine Light on the shadows that we hold inside ourselves, i.e. our emotional and psychological issues so that the latter can be released. So it's a very powerful mantra, used not only by Hindus but also by Buddhists and in yogic circles. It is so powerful that it is said that reciting the mantra will initiate a Second Birth, the first being our physical one, and the second, a spiritual one.

Thomas Ashley-Ferrand, in his book, *Healing Mantras* talks about an extended version of the mantra which is so long that he calls it a *freight-train mantra*. I personally use this version myself since the first seven Sanskrit words which point to the seven spheres of Light can be used in correspondence to the seven chakras so that they are easy to remember. Here it is in its long or full form:

*Om Bhuh, Om Bhuvaha, Om Swaha, Om Maha, Om Janaha, Om Tapaha, Om Satyam*
*Om Tat Savtur Varenyam, Bhargo devasya Dhimahi,*
*Dhiyo Yonaha Prachodayat*

(It has the same meaning as the English translation above.) There are some very beautiful recordings of the Gayatri. Many can be purchased easily through Indian cultural centres, yoga centres and the internet. Treat yourself to a CD which specifically has the Gayatri chanted and you can play it in your car or in your home until the mantra is ingrained in you and you can pick up its rhythm. I promise you, it will be worth your effort.

## Heal The World - Chant

It is no accident that churches, temples and mosques are peaceful places. The repetitive chanting of prayers has a very restful effect, not only on oneself but on one's surroundings. Therefore to make the world a better place, start by chanting a mantra of peace in whatever religious tradition you are comfortable with. In Sanskrit, it is *Om Shanti, Shanti*, Om Peace, Peace. In Tibetan it is *Om Mani Padme Hung*, the Jewel is in your Heart Lotus (for peace and compassion). Don't underestimate the power of a chant. Notice how old churches, temples and monasteries, even disused ones has the energy of peace with its walls or remaining walls. Energy can penetrate matter and is held within the atmosphere through time. Sense this for yourself. Once you have understood the potency of a mantra through your own experience, you will be more effective in wanting to generate the right energy to help change the world into a better place.

Conversely, sound uttered wrongly, in angry and hurtful tones; the human voice used to slander or blame has just as much power and effect as one used for good. Therefore the responsibility of someone who is on the path is to guard one's words with care, to use our voice only for good and the positive.

Besides the Gayatri Mantra, one Sanskrit mantra that is considered very powerful in self and universal healing is called the *Maharityunjaya Mantra* which is a practice that will help you to purify the karmas of the soul at a deep level and is beneficial for mental, emotional and physical health. This is also the mantra which will help you to attain Enlightenment.

179

*Om Trayambakam Yaja Mahe*
*Sugandhim Pushti Vardhanam*
*Urvar Ukamiva Bandhanna*
*Mrityor Mukshiya Mamritat*

*I take refuge in the three-eyed one*
*Fragrant and worthy of worship*
*Bless me and sever me from the clutches of death*
*Even as a cucumber is severed from its creeper*

This is indeed a very long mantra but has so many benefits that it is imperative to learn it. It benefits not yourself but the world and planet. Although it is generally said to eradicate diseases in one's body, it is believed in many circles that this mantra dispel social and universal maladies as well. I am particularly fond of this mantra as it has helped me through enormous challenges and gave me clarity of mind indicating to me my role and responsibility in the break-up of my marriages and the lessons I needed to learn from them.

Every time you chant a mantra for positive effect, you are posting new and positive energy to people and to the world. So if you want to help the environment, whether it is to help minimise the Greenhouse effect, the wars, natural disasters or whatever, chant! So heal yourself and others. Heal the world – chant!

# CHAPTER 14

# Don't Let Your Dreams Die

*"He whose face gives no light, shall never become a star"*
*- The Marriage Of Heaven & Hell*, William Blake

Many of us are wounded, in the grip of some kind of pain, either emotional, mental or physical. In one form or another, in one degree or another. Society too is wounded, in pain – you can see it in the violence that prevails, at home, in streets, in countries. Violence is not just physical; people inflict emotional and psychological violence too. Distress and anguish fill the columns of newspapers, blemish our television screens, films and books. Even the universe is wounded and in pain – look at what is happening to the air we breathe, to our trees, to our natural resources, to our world, our universe. We are largely in a sorry state of affairs.

Why? Because many of us are living in shadow. We have forgotten who we truly are. Too many people act like herd animals, doing what is expected by others so that we can fit into a particular group, belong to a certain club. Too many people sacrifice their sense of themselves in order not to be lonely. Many attach themselves to someone or something so that they feel less alone just so that they have the sense of belonging, possessing and being possessed. It's a kind of prostitution. It often means that they have to compromise. Compromise can be good, can be used to recognise another person's needs but it depends on the intention. Sometimes compromise is an opt-out and thus is not always a good thing. When you compromise, you sometimes let go of your dreams. And slowly, the non-fulfilment of your dreams starts to fester within you and you become a disgruntled person.

For example, if a woman gives up her dream of becoming an artist, a musician or a dancer to become a wife and mother, her non-fulfilment can injure herself and her family in later years because she felt she had given up what she loved for them, her sense of sacrifice is always with her – and she makes the family pay for it by over-demanding their love. Or a man gives up his life to work to keep his family in luxury but yet has no time to spend with them; in the end the family is dissatisfied with him and he in turn can't get the love he craves from them nor did he fulfil his dream of going skiing or canoeing in wild places. In the end, no one wins.

So don't let your dreams die. Someone once said:

*When dreams die, life is like a winged bird that cannot fly.*

This is not a passport to become selfish. The fulfilment of your dreams should take you nearer, not further away from The Divine. This is your yardstick. If the fulfilment of your dreams takes you further or away from The Divine, then they are dreams engendered by the Ego-self, not your Higher Self.

Look around you and you will see that too many people allow their dreams to die. It takes courage to fulfil your dreams. Sometimes people sacrifice their dreams for security of a warm bed, warm arms, friendship, good food, a good lifestyle. But if you have everything you want materially and are still not happy, it means that somehow you have let slip your Life's Purpose. This results in more and more people becoming unhappy, more and more are feeling unfulfilled. People are getting depressed, angrier, becoming more selfish. We become reliant on alcohol, smoking and other indulgent activities to provide us with sensual pleasures, to get us out of this rut of despair. We live vicarious lives through others, hence the Celebrity Culture, the so-called Reality TV. Yet living a secondary life also fills us with displeasure. The more we do, the more we find that we experience a core of loneliness and a bad after-taste of dissatisfaction. Our unhappiness is the real pollutant of this planet, not just carbon emissions. We are sending up clouds of negativity into the atmosphere. We have to correct this soon because the world cannot sustain this – our spirit cannot sustain this.

It is time for positive change.

You can make a difference.

## You Can Make A Difference

People are astonished when they are told that they can make the difference to the world. How can I, a puny thing, an unimportant, uninfluential person make a difference to the world, one might ask? But we can and we do. Not necessarily in a huge way. Not in the beginning anyway. But in our way, by our own small step. Imagine a dark room. Imagine this to be the state of the world, physically and metaphorically. Just by one person lighting up a single candle, she can lessen the darkness in this room. It seems such an obvious statement but its enormity is sometimes missed. If one person lights a candle, then gives the light to another person in the room, then turn to the next person to light up her candle and so forth, gradually the darkness in the room will be dispelled. Not by one huge floodlight that came on suddenly but slowly, with one single lighted candle. One person *can* make a difference. And that one person is you.

The moment we connect with The Divine, we have made a start to making a difference. You don't have to be Enlightened to make a difference. (To be Enlightened is like having the power of floodlights at a football stadium! This is the Gift of the few like Jesus Christ, Buddha, Guru Nanak and other Great Teachers.) The rest of us mortals are still struggling to find the switch! But, you can still make a difference even if your light in the beginning is weak because several weak points of light still make an impact on darkness. Imagine then the area of darkness you can dispel if the power of your light is turned on full. Imagine this wonderful glow of light surrounding our Universe. Your Light is manifested through positive thoughts, positive words and an enthusiasm for Real Life. When your Light is shining, it helps others to see through their shadows. What joy then when other pin-points of light of other awakening souls join your pin-point of light. More areas of darkness will be dispelled, making the world a better place

**Conversely**, negative thoughts, anger and selfishness too can influence the world and make a difference, but for the worse. Even one single bad thought from you can affect the world in a negative way. You do make a difference. Take a clear glass mixing bowl or jug. Fill it with pure spring water. Use a pipit and drop one drop of black ink into the water. Watch what happens. The ink darkens the water straight-away, then it spreads. That is how our negativity spreads as well. Once you accept that you, yes you, can make a difference, you would start feeling responsible for the condition of yourself, your world and the rest of the world by your thoughts and your actions. You try your best, as humanly possible, not to add to the storehouse of pain, hurt and negativity that is already out there. In fact your service is in lessening the impact of such adverse effects, whether it is to the personal or larger environment.

I would like to share with you one of my favourite sayings by the Buddha:

*The thought manifests as the word*
*The word manifests as deed*
*Deed develops into habit*
*Habit hardens into character*
*So watch the thought and its ways with care*
*Let it spring from love and concern for all beings*
*The shadow follows the body and never leaves it*
*In the same way, as we think, so we become*

*As we think, so we become* — This is how powerful our thoughts are. Our thoughts can shape us, can influence us, can make us happy, can make us sad. It is not so much the events outside ourselves that affect us but the events inside our mind that produce the greater effects. That is why many Eastern religions and philosophies like Buddhism and Yoga work towards developing a positive Mind and then eventually to be free of its hold on us. That is why, meditation is a very important aspect of spiritual growth. Meditation is time and space set aside for contemplation. This period of detachment from our daily life to enter into silence allows you to tune in, to what is happening within your Mind and your Body and also to tune in to The Divine.

But the Mind does not exist without the individual, it expresses itself through a human being, a human being who has a body. So if we can see how the Mind play tricks on the Body, and vice-versa, how the conditions of the Body affects the Mind, then we are able to distance ourselves from both and realise that we are actually more than just this Body or Mind, that we are in truth, Spirit. But don't take my word for it, or anybody's word for that matter, discover it for yourself. Nobody can tell you or give you their version of how to experience The Divine. What is in this book or other books are my words or other people's words or words borrowed from others, they can only take you to the brink of discovery of The Divine. You have to make the discovery yourself. There is only one way for you to know the real truth – and that is to know it for yourself.

## Transforming Yourself Is Your Service To The World

The one constant that we can be sure of is that change is part of living. Nothing remains static. We are in constant flux, from the micro to the macro level. At every single moment, our skin is changing, regenerating, so are our brain cells. This is the same outside ourselves, in the world and the universe. Fear stops us changing. Fear makes us cling to the familiar. This is the type of fear that people who need to remain artificially young forever have to deal with. We create the bogey-man with our Minds. Knowing that our body and our attitudes have to change is understanding the natural process. If we try to resist change, we will only encounter unhappiness. We will tend to live outdated lives, hold outdated ideas, cling to useless structures which seem to support us but are really leaning against nothing substantial.

If you are reading this far, you must have already sensed that there is another way to live your life. A way more significant where you can contribute to the world. Don't waste your energy trying to change others. Change yourself. Work on yourself. Then like a stone dropped into the edge of a pond, the ripples will spread to the far side of the pond. Change with good intent is a transformation. When you make a positive change, all else will transform around you, some things you may not see as positive in the beginning but which you will see as necessary in retrospect. The effects of your change will be far-reaching. Changing yourself for the better is your service to the world. Some people are destined to live in the mountains, monasteries or ashrams in their service to the world. The majority of us are not. We need not run away from society, our service is in the community, practising our spirituality in everyday life, doing our best in our daily work and interaction. Spirituality can and is more pragmatic than people think. As we said in the introduction, using your gifts that you are born with is a good way of contributing to society. When you are using your gifts, you become alive – and it is your aliveness and vitality which generate aliveness in others. If you obstruct your creativity, you become unfulfilled. If you don't go with the flow and rhythm of life, you will be inert, like dead wood. If you only exist and don't live, you will be part of the living dead – going through the motions of life but not living.

The wisdom to know what changes to make cannot be forced from the intellect and ego or Operating Personality. It has to come from an inner understanding, from your intuition, from an ancient wisdom, from your connection to the Divine. The latter is a result of the work you do on your chakras or gateways to The Divine. Part of the change that results from working on yourself is the new understanding that we are all inter-connected beings. In Chapter 2 when we spoke of separateness of countries and bodies, we saw how a different perspective showed that at a different level, countries are not really separate nor are bodies if we see that at a pranic level, our Consciousness are not separate. So in changing ourselves, we are helping in the change of this Consciousness. We are helping to hold the Light for others. When you are doing what you love, in honour of The Divine, then you will be transforming yourself and make your vocation a service to the world. This is True Spirituality, living your life whilst being connected to The Divine so that your everyday activities take on a deeper meaning. The Dalai Lama, on his October 31st meditation, in his book of daily meditation said, "*Through actual practise in his daily life, man well fulfils the aim of all religions, whatever his denomination.*"

## Dark Night of The Soul

Don't think that getting on the Path is an easy option. It is not. That is why spiritual aspirants are called *Warriors of Light*. Paulo Coelho said, in his *Manual Of The Warrior Of Light*, "A warrior of light is never cowardly." You have to be courageous and you have to fight to gain the Light – battles within and without. Every spiritual aspirant will tell you that she has encountered periods which have been tough and at some point was unsure if she was on the Path. This is the *dark night of the soul*. The latter are not my words. It is a phrase borrowed from St. John of The Cross, a 16th Century Carmelite priest and mystic to describe the loneliness and desolation one feels at one stage of the spiritual journey. The phrase is the name of his poem and theological commentary and it expresses the challenging process of letting go of one's ego to make room for some form of transformation. There are two stages during this period of the *dark night*, the first being the purification of the senses and second, the purification of the spirit. In working through our chakras which are connected with our senses, we are purifying our senses which will lead us to purifying our spirit.

Every religious tradition has spoken of this *dark night of the soul*, a period of uncertainty which seems like a testing. Jesus Christ experienced this in the Garden of Gethsemane, just before Judas came to identify him. He asked for the *Cup* to pass from him. He was at his lowest ebb in spiritual trust and at one point on the cross, he did cry out to God, "Father, why has thou forsaken me?"

The *dark night of the soul* does feel like one has been abandoned. But it is not a test that some Divine God has meted out to you. It's your own soul working through the rubbish that has been accumulated in this and several life-times. If you like, it is like our karmic debt, solely owed by ourselves and no other. This period reveals to us our weaknesses and obstacles that we have put in the way of our spiritual progress. Without learning of our weaknesses and overcoming them, our strength and power cannot surface. We cannot carry the torch that makes us *Warriors of Light*. As the Tibetan saying at the beginning of this book says,

*If you want to know what you were doing in your Past Life,*
*look at what your present body is like now*

Your present body and mind give you indication of what had gone one before. That is why witnessing our body and mind is imperative for spiritual development. At this point, it might seem that everything is against you despite the fact that you have meditated, given up this-and-that, lived a life of purity, etc. etc. You tend to experience a loss of some kind in some kind of way: a spouse, a partner, money, a home, a job, a way of life or whatever is important to you. But you are not the first. Even the Buddha experienced this. After having given up his position and kingdom, wealth, his luxury life-style in his palace, his family, he did not find Enlightenment straightaway. He was said to be besieged by *demons* or *mara*, in Sanskrit, which we now come to understand was his period of the *dark night of the soul*. But he never gave up. He not only found Enlightenment, his Light is so strong that he gave it to others, and continue to give to others through his teachings.

However, in the spiritual scheme of things, the period of the *dark night of the soul* is definitely temporary. However, St. Paul of the Cross claimed that his dark night lasted 45 years and Mother Theresa of Calcutta said hers lasted till her death with periods of respite in-between. Yet in relation to eternity, this is still considered temporary. But don't let it demoralise you. It's important to recognise this stage in order to overcome it. A lump of coal lies in the dark earth for years, being compressed physically as it goes through a process of chemical transformation. If the lump of coal has any sensory impulses then surely this is the period when it would experience most pressure. Then it is unearthed to see daylight and has to be grind (experiencing pain) to be shaped into a beautiful, sparkling diamond. Our soul too has to go through a similar process. The period of the *dark night of the soul* is painful. But like Kahlil Gibran said in *The Prophet*, the pain that you suffer, *"is the breaking of the shell that encloses your understanding."* The process, like the transformation of the piece of coal into diamond, is gruelling but will clear the dross that is in us so that arrive at a new understanding of what IS. It is then that we are transformed into our spiritual, sparkling diamond and its Light can shine forth. See this period of the *dark night* as a positive progression of your soul. There is not much point in your learning all the spiritual principles from gurus, books and going to retreats if you don't practise what you have learnt. The ultimate test of whether you have truly learnt is whether you can walk your talk. This period of the *dark night of the soul* is the period where what you have learnt has to be put into real everyday practice. When you have refined your way of tuning in to the frequency and wave-band of The Divine and once you get the wave-band right you will never lose the connection to The Divine; and even if you did, in moments of high emotional static, you can recapture it back quickly.

Unlike the inert lump of coal, we as human beings who can exercise free-will have a participatory part to play during this dark period. We can choose to give in and give up or we can choose to persevere to liberate ourselves from the ignorance and falsity of our previous lives to live the Real Life. Although we might feel that we have been abandoned during this difficult time, we are not. We have to resort to the help of The Divine. Instead of despairing and letting go of our spiritual practices, this is the period when we need them most. Some of the form might change, for example, during this period, it might be difficult, even impossible to do a seated meditation, so do a meditation-in-action. Develop love and compassion for yourself and for others. Use mantras to call for Divine succour and keep focusing on the rainbow in you. Have the courage to go through the throes of labour-pain to birth a new you. Also call upon others who share the Path, a community of like-minded people, who like you are opening up the gateways in their body, bringing out their rainbows. This community is what the Buddhists call a *sangha*, a group of people who can understand or who have experienced the trials you are experiencing. These are the people who are holding the Light for the world and who share your spiritual dreams and aspirations.

## Emergence Of A Spiritual Community

This chapter began on a slightly negative note with an observation of the sorry state of affairs of our societal conditions. Perhaps our current milieu is a symbol of the whole world too undergoing its *dark night of the soul*. Therefore this period can be seen as positive as there is promise of better things to come. You can already see it happening. Only through experiencing the dark side of life can we be propelled towards the Light of Source or The Divine. We must participate in assisting the world to pass its *dark night* for it to emerge into Light.

Religious dogmas tend to focus on our conscience on what is right or wrong in relation to an ascribed God. Therefore their dogmas have to be prescriptive to have any influence and whack. Such rigidity does not embrace the difference in expression of other creeds as other prescriptions from other creeds become a threat to their own. But when spiritual principles are based on tapping into a Universal Consciousness, there is no need to be prescriptive since the perception of that Consciousness can be individual providing no threat to another's belief. If we adopt this attitude, then all religions can exist in harmony, people can exist in harmony, respecting each other's ways of expressing The Divine in each other's lives.

Technological advancement may be a human achievement and success but it is largely focused on matter and the more gross elements of our existence. Whilst there are undeniable benefits, there are also grave implications to our emotional, psychological and spiritual growth. It takes us out of nature into the micro and cyber-world of transient and imagined avatars and life-styles. Just think how ludicrous it is that an internet company has managed to set up a cyber-world and managed to persuade people to reinvent themselves as Avatars, buy cyber-land and properties and set up cyber businesses to live their lives in cyber relationships with cyber-identities who do not actually exist in real-time space. This is truly madness and can only be that we have lost our sense of perspective and are experiencing the dark night of our soul! (I particularly dislike the misuse of the word *avatar* since it used to mean a spiritual deity taking human form. There is no spiritual element in a cyber-avatar since the world they inhabit is one where the Ego-Self or Operating Personality's desires and needs are being fulfilled and nothing else.) We lose touch with what is real and our human, societal interaction become impaired. That is why holistic spirituality returns us to nature-based traditions because a re-connection to the healing properties and energy of the natural universe is imperative for our Real Development. Working on our seven chakras or gateways that are within our body will provide us with the mystical insight necessary to perceive that the world of cyber-space is false and the world of spirit is more real.

Fortunately, all is not lost. Disillusionment and dissatisfaction of the superficiality of the current fabric of the world has spearheaded many people towards searching for meaning in their lives. We have to be careful not to make this search another goal, like all the other empirical goals that our Ego or Operating Personality demands of us. This search is an approach rather than a method. It is a day-to-day manner of living holistically. It takes us inward and not outward. No displays or outward show of this search is necessary. It is a commendation to our humanity that there is an emergence of a spiritual community who does care about the state and condition of themselves, others, the world and the universe. It is due to these people that there is still hope for the world. In the words of the Dalai Lama, from his 15th December advice in his *Book of Daily Meditations, "Mankind is crying out for help. Ours is a desperate time. Those who have something to offer should come forward. Now is the time."*

## Be A Star!

Indeed, when you have taken time to work on the Seven Gateways of your body to The Divine, you will be ready to carry out the primary purpose of your being here in this life-time – to fulfil your Life's Purpose. Every one has a Life Purpose. This is not a vocation of the Ego –Self or Operating Personality but of your Soul. It will not be something outside your ability or perimeters in that it is your own calling and you came into this incarnation laden with the gifts to do so. The fact that you may have forgotten or mislaid your gifts in the process of living a life that has not made you happy does not mean that the resources are not within you. You have to trust. But the more you work on yourself and strengthen the connection to The Divine, that trust will come. You just need to get away form the path that leads you into the tangled woods and you will see the clearing and a way out. Ultimately it is down to your choice. Your true happiness depends on it. Your future is indeed in your hands. Being on the Path means that you accept your life as your responsibility and the challenges your Soul have to face. There is no escape by trying to blame someone else for your Life's outcome. That is why it requires tremendous strength and courage to be a *Warrior of Light*. As the Tibetan saying at the front of this book states,

*If you want to know what will happen to you in your Future Life, look at what your present mind is doing now*

Make sure that your Mind is setting up the right future for you. In the same way that you are careful to find an insurance policy which will give you the right benefits when you are old, make sure that your Present Mind is accruing the right circumstances for your Future life. A peaceful mind which is not pulled away by the steeds of desire, anger and avarice is a mind ruled by the True Self. In awakening to Consciousness, you are laying the foundations for a Divine connection and for your future Light-Enhancing moments. Then joy, equanimity and abundance will be yours.

As William Blake said, *He whose face gives no light, cannot be a star.* By *star*, we obviously don't mean the celluloid, Hollywoodian type which has no real glow but the kind of star that shines with celestial light. Celestial light cast away shadows. Work on your chakras and open the gateways in your body to receive The Divine Light and your light will shine forth from you and you will be truly a star!

As I was working on this book and focusing on the idea of the rainbow in ourselves, I kept seeing rainbows everywhere. And though I am not musically literate and cannot read or write music, a song came to me! Complete with words and a tune, the first song I ever composed! I am unable to tell you the song in musical notes though I hope some day a musically talented someone will tell me and write it out so that others can sing it too. (Let me know if you are the one.) But I can sing it and share it with you by giving you the lyrics:

Rainbows Everywhere
*There are rainbows everywhere*
*In drops of water, in the air*
*Caught in light and bits of glass*
*Sparkling colours just for us*

*Yet we turn our eyes away*
*Blindly going through our day*
*Caught in pain and misery*
*Painting black our history*

*See the rainbows everywhere*
*In drops of water, in the air*
*Break away from misery,*
*let the colours set you free*
*Break away from misery,*
*let the colours set you free*

I hope one day I will have the opportunity to sing my song to you. I hope we can meet and celebrate the fact that you have opened the gateways in your body to The Divine and the rainbow will be brilliant in your aura. Your face will be suffused with celestial light and you will shine brightly like the star that you are.

# ACKNOWLEDGEMENTS OF PUBLICATIONS FOR USE OF QUOTATIONS

| Title Of Book/Author | Publisher/Year | ISBN |
|---|---|---|
| *Health & Hatha Yoga* Swami Sivananda, Life And Works Of Swami Sivananda Volume 2 | Divine Life Society 1985 | 0-949027-03-0 |
| *To Know Your Self* *The Essential Teachings Of* *Swami Satchidananda,* Edited by Philip Mandelkorn | Anchor Books Anchor Press New York | 0-385-1261311978 |
| *Henry V* William Shakespeare | | |
| *The Bhagavad Gita,* With a commentary based on the original sources by R.C. Zaehner | Oxford University Press 1969 | 0-19-501666-1 |
| *A Blessing For The Senses* *Anam Cara,* John O'Donohue | Bantam books 1997 | 0-553-50592-0 |
| **The Book Of Job, Bible** | | |
| *Handbook to Higher* *Consciousness,* Ken Keyes, Jr. | Living Love Publications, US 1985 | 978-09600-68883 |

| | | |
|---|---|---|
| *Creativity, Unleashing The*<br>*Forces Within*<br>Osho | St. Martin's Griffin<br>1999 | 0-312-20519-8 |
| *The Art Of Living*<br>*A guide to contentment, joy*<br>*and fulfillment*<br>His Holiness, The Dalai Lama | Thorsons, imprint of<br>Harper Collins | 0-00-766981-X |
| *Spiritual Growth,*<br>*Being Your Higher Self*<br>Sanaya Roman | HJ Kramer Inc<br>California  1989 | 0-915811-12-X |
| *The Intuitive Way,*<br>*A Guide To Living From*<br>*Inner Wisdom*<br>Penney Peirce | Beyond Words<br>Publishing 1997 | 1-84013-511-5 |
| *Blake, Complete Writings*<br>William Blake | Oxford University<br>Press 1972 | 0-19-281050-2 |
| *The Dalai Lama's Book Of*<br>*Daily Mediations*<br>*The Path To Tranquillity*<br>Compiled and edited by Renuka Singh | Rider , Random<br>House Group 1998 | 0-7126-0898-2 |
| *Healing Mantras, Using*<br>*Sound Affirmations For*<br>*Personal Power, Creativity*<br>*And Healing*<br>Thomas Ashley-Farrand | Gateway 2000,<br>An imprint of Gill &<br>Macmillan Ltd | 0-7171-3001-0 |

# BOOKS

O is a symbol of the world, of oneness and unity. In different cultures it also means the "eye", symbolizing knowledge and insight. We aim to publish books that are accessible, constructive and that challenge accepted opinion, both that of academia and the "moral majority".

Our books are available in all good English language bookstores worldwide. If you don't see the book on the shelves ask the bookstore to order it for you, quoting the ISBN number and title. Alternatively you can order online (all major online retail sites carry our titles) or contact the distributor in the relevant country, listed on the copyright page.

See our website www.o-books.net for a full list of over 400 titles, growing by 100 a year.

And tune in to myspiritradio.com for our book review radio show, hosted by June-Elleni Laine, where you can listen to the authors discussing their books.

mySpiritRadio